Simone Weil's Political Philosophy

Simone Weil's Political Philosophy

Field Notes from the Margins

Benjamin P. Davis

ROWMAN & LITTLEFIELD
Lanham • Boulder • New York • London

Published by Rowman & Littlefield
An imprint of The Rowman & Littlefield Publishing Group, Inc.
4501 Forbes Boulevard, Suite 200, Lanham, Maryland 20706
www.rowman.com

86-90 Paul Street, London EC2A 4NE

British Library Cataloguing in Publication Information Available

Library of Congress Cataloging-in-Publication Data

Library of Congress Cataloging-in-Publication DataNames: Davis, Benjamin P., author.
 Title: Simone Weil's political philosophy : field notes from the margins /
  Benjamin P. Davis.
 Description: Lanham, Maryland : Rowman & Littlefield, [2023] | Includes
  bibliographical references and index. | Summary: "Davis demonstrates how
  Simone Weil's Marxism challenges current neoliberal understandings of
  the self and of human rights. Explaining her related critiques of
  colonialism and of political parties, it presents Weil as a
  twentieth-century political philosopher who anticipated and critically
  responded to the most contemporary political theory"-- Provided by
  publisher.
 Identifiers: LCCN 2022052208 (print) | LCCN 2022052209 (ebook) | ISBN
  9781538171943 (Cloth) | ISBN 9781538171967 (epub)
 Subjects: LCSH: Weil, Simone, 1909-1943--Political and social views.
 Classification: LCC B2430.W474 D298 2023 (print) | LCC B2430.W474 (ebook)
  | DDC 194--dc23/eng/20230206
 LC record available at https://lccn.loc.gov/2022052208
 LC ebook record available at https://lccn.loc.gov/2022052209

To Rebecca, Lucian, Scott, and Helen

Contents

Acknowledgments

I have looked forward to the moment in which I could publicly thank those who have shaped this book: Scott Ritner, for asking me in Boston to elaborate on how I read Weil. Lissa McCullough, for such strikingly original and illuminating readings of Weil. Caleb Faul, Gary Suchor, Carlie Hughes, and Jaclyn Berg, for formative conversations, and for our efforts to challenge a neoliberal university. Beatrice Marovich, for lending me so many books. The librarians of Emory University and the University of Toronto, for getting me Weil's work in French. The security staff at Emory's Woodruff Library, especially C.J., for letting me into my study to read Weil before the stacks were supposed to be open. My parents and brother, for lifelong support. Sophie Bourgault, for her reading of Weil as a figure of care, and for living out that ethic. Andrew Tyler Johnson, for reading all my work. Eric Aldieri, for an infinite conversation. Baruch Malewich, for pointing out tensions in Weil's critique of collectivity. Christy Wampole, for teaching me about the essay. Valérie Loichot, for encouraging me to read Weil alongside Glissant. Adam Sitze, for reading so well. Cindy Willett and John Lysaker, for reading my manuscript-sized early reflections on Weil. John Stuhr, for pluralistic disagreement. Tom Flynn, for asking me to write an encyclopedia entry on Weil. Fannie Bialek, for asking me to read Weil with her, and for showing me how to read better. Diane Enns, for returning me to Weil's early work. Penny Weiss, for conversation. Miguel Gualdrón Ramírez, por todo. Lauren Highsmith, for what you do, and for your music. Chelsea Jack, for your thoughts. Rohini Patel, for conversation about Weil over wine. Mark Kingwell, for mentorship. Vincent Lloyd, for mentorship. Lucy Benjamin, for encouragement. Frieda Ekotto, for reminding me that we read Weil for the depth of her thinking. Jessica Whyte, for compelling conversation. Gerard Aching, for showing me how to live well. Gabby, for being who you are. Lucian, for keeping your door open. Helen, for living a feminist life. Rebecca, for teaching me to write.

Author's Note

When reading commentary on a translation, it is my preference as a reader to have citations of both the translation and the original in the body of the text. As much as possible, in this book I provided references to both, listing the English/French page numbers. That is the good news. The bad news is that this book was written entirely during the COVID-19 pandemic. As a result, I had limited access to academic libraries, so I relied on online sources more than I would have otherwise. When I cited the original French versions of Weil's texts, I relied on the editions found in the French digital library of Les Classiques des sciences sociales, which is associated with l'Université du Québec à Chicoutimi. I cited the page numbers that can be found on the top right corner of each digitalized page.

Abbreviations

APP *On the Abolition of All Political Parties*. Translated by Simon Leys. New York: New York Review of Books, 2013.

CO *La condition ouvrière*. Paris: Éditions Gallimard, 1951.

EHP *Écrits historiques et politiques*. Paris: Éditions Gallimard, 1960.

EL *Écrits de Londres et dernières lettres*. Paris: Éditions Gallimard, 1957.

EM *Écrits de Marseille*. Paris: Éditions Gallimard, 2008.

FW *Formative Writings: 1929–1941*. Translated by Dorothy Tuck McFarland and Wilhelma Van Ness. Amherst: University of Massachusetts Press, 1987.

GG *Gravity and Grace*. Translated by Emma Crawford and Mario von der Ruhr. New York: Routledge, 2002; *La Pesanteur et la grâce*. Paris: Librairie Plon, 1947.

LPW *Simone Weil: Late Philosophical Writings*. Translated by Eric O. Springsted and Lawrence E. Schmidt. Notre Dame: University of Notre Dame Press, 2015.

NR *The Need for Roots*. Translated by Arthur Wills. New York: Routledge, 2002; *L'enracinement. Prélude à une déclaration des devoirs envers l'être humain*. Paris: Éditions Gallimard, 1949.

OL *Oppression and Liberty*. Translated by Arthur Wills and John Petrie. New York: Routledge, 1958; *Oppression et liberté*. Paris: Éditions Gallimard, 1955.

SE *Selected Essays 1934–1943: Historical, Political, and Moral Writings*. Translated by Richard Rees. Eugene: Wipf and Stock, 2015.

SS   *Sur la science.* Paris: Éditions Gallimard, 1966.
SWA   *Simone Weil: An Anthology.* New York: Penguin, 2005.
SWC   *Simone Weil on Colonialism.* Translated and edited by J. P.
          Little. Lanham: Rowman & Littlefield, 2003.
WG   *Waiting for God.* Translated by Emma Craufurd. New York:
          Routledge Revivals, 2009; *Attente de Dieu.* Paris: Éditions
          Fayard, 1966.

Preface

Simone Weil's life and work continue to speak to me so strongly because of how she tried to live ethically in her complicated and compromised time, a time of capitalism and empire that remains our time, that reaches into the present. It was not that she simply sought to be a "good person"—she knew that by living comfortably in France, a colonizing country, she was too complicit in state-based practices of domination to claim such a title for herself. Instead of making such claims, she asked questions—of herself, of others, and of the world. I remain compelled by her practice of inquiry that involves not only reading as much as she could from a variety of traditions—she would learn Sanskrit in order to appreciate with more nuance the *Bhagavad Gita*—but also testing her insights in practice, reflecting on that practice in writing that we might call her field notes, and essaying those ideas in practice again. Indeed, Weil's sense of essaying was never limited to writing; it was also about honoring the conversations she had before and after her pen touched the page. She consistently tried to learn from those who had *lived* the concepts. When she studied oppression, she placed herself amidst Parisian factory workers. When she studied labor, she picked grapes in French vineyards. Through a class analysis, Weil's actions could be understood as patronizing, being that she came from a wealthy family. But when we also consider that she came from a Jewish family and lived in an anti-Semitic society, and that she was a woman living in a patriarchal society, it is our clear-cut diagnoses and categorizations of her life that become troubled. What we are left with is a philosopher who grappled seriously, rigorously, and intelligently with her responsibilities to others in a context of tremendous brutality. When she is understood that way, Simone Weil becomes our teacher in the present.

Benjamin P. Davis
Tkaronto/Toronto, Canada
January 2022

Introduction

Simone Weil as a Political Philosopher

Simone Weil's political philosophy attempted both to interpret and to change the world. Throughout her life, she remained critical of the nation-state and capitalism. "One cannot disregard the fact," she wrote incisively in her 1933 essay "Prospects," "that all the political currents which now affect the masses, whether they style themselves fascist, socialist, or communist, tend towards the same form of State capitalism" (OL 18/23). She also continually worked to transform her native France into a more just country. That work included organizing labor, teaching Sophocles, Plato, and Marx, living modestly, and dressing, as one of her biographers puts it, in "the clothes of a ragtag soldier or a poor monk," in garments "always of the same monastic, masculine cut."[1] In this way, her political philosophy involved both theory and practice.

This book is about Simone Weil's ideas. It is also about how she tested those ideas in the world. It is about the questions she asked, how she asked them, and whom she considered her audience. It is also about why she found some questions helpful and others limiting, why she used some concepts and discarded others, and how her method of testing ideas alongside workers and immigrants led her to draw some conclusions and not others about politics. In *Simone Weil's Political Philosophy*, I bring to the fore Weil's political writings, which in the United States are studied less than her theological writings. In each chapter, respectively, I put Weil into conversation with feminist philosophy, decolonial philosophy, aesthetic theory, human rights discourse, and Marxism.

* * *

Perhaps the largest barrier in the way of studying both Weil's ideas and how she tested them is how her life has already been described as interesting but ultimately as crazy. In a letter to her parents dated July 18, 1943, one of the last letters she wrote in her short life, she predicted this reception, expressing concern that people would focus on her attributes instead of reading her work

1

with patience, effort, and attention (EL 228–229). Of the ever-increasing number of biographical sketches of Weil easily found on the internet, many continue to play the role that biography has too often played regarding women philosophers: to treat their lives at the expense of their ideas, or to use their biography to invalidate their ideas. It was not so different in her own time; many people spoke about her in terms that overlooked her contributions as a political philosopher.

In the French context, several prominent writers described Weil in religious terms. Albert Camus called her "the only great spirit of our time," André Gide said she was "the patron saint of all outsiders," and Georges Bataille modeled a character—a sort of Christian revolutionary—after her in his novel *Blue of Noon*. Among philosophers, Maurice Blanchot praised Weil's thinking as "worthy of attention and rich in truth,"[2] and Emmanuel Levinas said she "lived like a saint and bore the suffering of the world."[3] General and President Charles de Gaulle simply called her "crazy."[4] Even her friends and biographers, Dominican priest Joseph-Marie Perrin and philosopher Gustave Thibon, used her habit of smoking as a point of contrast to say that she eschewed the basic goods of everyday life: "Of all the things belonging to material life, tobacco was the only one which she was almost certain to accept."[5] Later, philosopher Jean-François Lyotard, writing about philosophy in France as well as about Plato and Marx, arguably Weil's two greatest influences, simply did not mention her in his 1964 lectures to first-year philosophy students in Paris.[6]

Beyond the French context, readings of Weil vary widely. Some European philosophers found great value in her work. Hannah Arendt noted that perhaps only Weil treated the subject of labor "without prejudice and sentimentality."[7] Giorgio Agamben called her conscience "the most lucid of our times."[8] Writer Flannery O'Connor described Weil as a person of "great courage" whose life was both comic and terrible—in a word, "ridiculous."[9] Perhaps most famously, writing in *The New York Review of Books* one year before Lyotard's lectures, Susan Sontag described Weil's life as "absurd in its exaggerations and degree of self-mutilation," noting that it is a life to regard "from a distance with a mixture of revulsion, pity, and reverence."[10] Sontag continued: "We read writers of such scathing originality for their personal authority, for the example of their seriousness, for their manifest willingness to sacrifice themselves for their truths, and—only piecemeal—for their 'views.'"

In my attempt to focus on what Sontag describes as Weil's rarely considered "views," I aim to avoid two tendencies in writing about Weil that philosophers commenting on her work often fall back on. The first tendency is to portray her as a genius. For instance, Martin Andic comments on Henry Leroy Finch's writings on Weil: "[Finch] was convinced that Simone Weil is the genius we need to show us how to rethink religion, politics, history, and culture."[11] In my view, to argue that a single philosopher can guide contemporary society in seemingly all spheres of life overstates the importance of one thinker.

The second tendency is to stress the unity of Weil's work across space and time. For instance, Robert Chenavier argues that Weil's writings contain "an interior need for coherence, even if her work did not take the form of a system."[12] He goes on to extend this claim to other aspects of Weil's life: "To an exceptional degree, the life of Simone Weil, her personality, her commitment, and her reflection form one single whole."[13] While Weil's ability to connect her theoretical reflections to her political commitments is certainly inspiring, the tendency to view her work in terms of unity and wholeness, like the tendency to portray her as a genius, can have the effect of suggesting that she is a saint above basic human insight and contradiction. It is not necessarily the case that a few comments on Weil's coherence means that the commentator thinks she is a saint. But it is the case that such comments lend themselves to being read that way, leading some readers and students of Weil's work to underemphasize the internal tensions of her thought. To give just one example of these tensions, Weil begins *The Need for Roots* by juxtaposing contrary needs of the soul, maintains at once a critical and a constructive approach to political collectives throughout the book, and writes that text at the same time as she makes opposing arguments in *On the Abolition of All Political Parties*. In other words, her thought forms not a single whole but multiple parts.

Countering both of the above tendencies, in her 1988 *Between the Human and the Divine: The Political Thought of Simone Weil*, political theorist Mary Dietz locates in Weil's life and thought "a perpetual struggle" between "attachment and withdrawal, worldliness and worldlessness, the human and the divine."[14] Reading ambiguity into Weil's work, Dietz argues that Weil's later writings that suggest a withdrawal from the world are simply "the other side of her deep involvement in it."[15] Along similar lines, philosopher of religion Lissa McCullough explains that there are, in fact, two movements in Weil's religious philosophy, a dialectic constituted by (1) a transcendence of the finite through detachment and (2) a return to the finite through compassion.[16] Cultural theorist Deborah Nelson further observes that expecting Weil's writings to show excessive spiritual sentiment leads to the takeaway that Weil is another woman writer who is "psychologically cold rather than engaged in an ethical project with different assumptions."[17] Where Dietz, McCullough, and Nelson overlap is in their guiding effort to think about Weil in terms, to use political theorist Sophie Bourgault's phrase, "beyond the saint and the red virgin."[18] To see Weil as actively working between withdrawal from the world and engagement in it implies the need to read not only her theological writings but also her political writings. Dietz explicitly argues that "to understand Weil fully we need to attend not only to those writings that have already made her famous—her theological and mystical tracts, but also to those political writings that capture the 'other side' of her intellectual and practical life."[19] Only through this dual reading, Dietz concludes, can we understand what Weil offers contemporary political discourse.

In addition to returning to Dietz's book, today's students of Weil benefit from more recent books that explain and comment on Weil as a philosopher, including A. Rebecca Rozelle-Stone and Lucian Stone's *Simone Weil and Theology* and Lissa McCullough's *The Religious Philosophy of Simone Weil: An Introduction*. Further, Yoon Sook Cha illuminatingly connects Weil's theological orientation to practical ethics in *Decreation and the Ethical Bind: Simone Weil and the Claim of the Other*, Lewis Gordon links Weil's concept of decreation to political responsibility in *Fear of Black Consciousness*, and Vincent Lloyd, in *The Problem with Grace: Reconfiguring Political Theology*, reads Weil as making important contributions to political life.[20] "Weil seems to fit very easily into perversion as a diagnostic category," Lloyd helpfully warns.[21] If I follow his warning in this book, I depart from his claim that turning to her political writings is "counterproductive" because "Weil's political writings are political rhetoric, not political philosophy."[22] Lloyd's claim is indicative of a larger trend. Indeed, since Dietz's 1988 *Between the Human and the Divine*, readers in English are left with few options for studying how Weil's political philosophy contributes to new debates. If we follow Dietz's claim that to understand Weil's contributions for the present, we need to read her theological writings with her political writings, then readers of the aforementioned books would benefit from a text that focuses anew on Weil's "other side." In writing *Simone Weil's Political Philosophy*, I have aimed to provide that book.

* * *

Taking as my focus how her analysis of collective life (i.e. political life) shifted over time, in this book, I show how Weil's political philosophy contributes to ongoing political dilemmas. Each chapter examines a different stage of her lifelong critical relationship to what she calls "collectivity." By "collectivity," she means a basic group of social life such as a political party, church, trade union, government bureaucracy, or social movement. At present, many political actors are raising questions about the relationship they should cultivate with respect to the collectivities to which they belong. For instance, feminist philosophers debate the merits of the vocabulary of "resilience" or "resistance" in regard to political movements; like Weil in her 1934 essay "Reflections Concerning the Causes of Liberty and Social Oppression," they are interrogating the political vocabulary of their time. Similarly, when authors who have written for *Jacobin* worry about its affiliation with the

Democratic Party and start to write for the Marxist magazine *Left Voice*, they are calling into question any comfortable relationship with reformist political parties, as Weil did in her 1943 essay *On the Abolition of All Political Parties*. And when residents of Minneapolis consider how to rebuild their city following the occupation of the National Guard, they are raising questions about the relationship citizens should cultivate amongst one another post-occupation, as did Weil in her final book, *The Need for Roots*.

Weil observed that modern collectivities suffer from a lack of thinking. Surrounded by and forced to work within mechanical operations in industrial society, citizens themselves start to approximate machines instead of thinking for themselves. The political problem with this kind of unthinking is that it "tends pretty well everywhere toward a form of totalitarian organization" (OL 109/108). In other words, Weil specifies, unthinking members of a collective form the backbone of "a system in which the State power comes to exercise sovereign sway in all spheres, even, indeed above all, in that of thought [*surtout dans le domaine de la pensée*]" (OL 109/108). Weil would test these claims alongside other workers at a factory making electrical equipment for trams and railways. This historical detail provides a contrast with the often-painted image of Weil as the great figure of withdrawal from the world, epitomized in the subtitle to a 2022 *New York Review of Books* essay, which read "Simone Weil's political and moral vision always looked beyond her own earthly sphere of existence, which she held in more or less steady contempt."[23] What literary theorist Lyndsey Stonebridge observes in writing about Weil and human rights serves as a guiding claim throughout this book: "Weil wanted to get as far into her world as possible."[24]

The overarching contention of this book is that that Weil's critical relationship to collectivity and unyielding criticism of social life in her oppressive context stems not from genius, saintliness, or illness but from the fact that she was a philosopher. With Socrates principally in mind, historian of philosophy Pierre Hadot writes that the figure of the philosopher in ancient Greece was *atopos*, meaning "out of place."[25] With Hegel, Marx, and Nietzsche in mind, and assessing the past and future of Critical Theory, philosopher Nikolas Kompridis writes that being a philosopher means "being out of step with, in contradiction to, one's time, forced to oppose it, and to act as its 'bad conscience.'"[26] In the history of Western philosophy, both ancient and modern, then, philosophical life has involved a critique of the world as it is. For that reason, we do not necessarily need any hyperbolic or psychoanalytic explanations for Weil's interrogations of the self, the social, and the world. The answer might lie simply in the fact that she was a philosopher.

Further, Weil fits into the definitions prominent philosophers have used to think about political philosophy. For instance, philosopher James Tully has defined political philosophy as

> a critical attitude [that] starts from the present struggles and problems of politics and seeks to clarify and transform the normal understanding of them so as to open up the field of possible ways of thinking and acting freely in response . . . By studying the unanticipated blockages, difficulties, and new problems that arise in the cycle of practices of freedom—of negotiations, implementations, and review—political philosophers can detect the limitations and faults of their initial account, make improvements, and exercise again, on the basis of the new problems, this permanent critical *ethos* of testing the practices by which we are governed.[27]

Tully has in mind Michel Foucault in particular, but we could very well think of Weil as exemplary of his definition. Keeping in mind Hadot's reading of the philosopher as *atopos*, I see Weil as a philosopher; keeping in mind Tully's definition of political philosophy as a "critical attitude," I read Weil as a political philosopher.

Some will immediately dismiss my claim—Weil as a political philosopher—as a misreading of a thinker who wanted so clearly to excise certain elements of herself, who had little tolerance for ambiguity and instead sought purity. When I look at the footnotes backing up those claims in the scholarly literature, or when I ask scholars at conferences how they arrived at the conclusion that Weil was mentally ill, they tend to cite her notebooks, letters to friends, or the "terrible prayer," which she wrote in her New York notebooks.[28] They also tend not to engage Weil's early writings on politics. While I do not want to police the boundaries of philosophy proper—and certainly notebook entries can be philosophical—I have come to wonder how fair it is to make sweeping and indeed damning conclusions about a person and a life based on their most personal, tentative writings. I maintain that, whereas a published article is a place to demonstrate a clear voice, a journal or notebook is a place of immense vulnerability. It is a place where we explore our own depths.[29] Reading Weil as a fellow traveler, as human all too human like the rest of us, we can start to consider her contradictory claims less as part of an epic battle between gravity and grace and more as reflective of a person with the courage to consider—and often hold together in what the poet John Keats called "negative capability"—the tremendous anxieties and contradictions that face any person who tarries with the questions that emerge from a robust confrontation with modern political life.[30] Blanchot puts it this way: "I do not see why Simone Weil alone would be disqualified as a thinker because she accepted within herself as legitimate the inevitable opposition of thoughts."[31]

What we gain from reading Weil as a fellow traveler—if, admittedly, an idiosyncratic one—is both an ability to criticize her limitations honestly and an opening to learn from her dynamic use of concepts, claims, and questions. My approach is thus different from tendencies to read Weil either as offering a path holier than the one on which her reader is currently walking or as pathological. In regard to the tendency to say she offers a holy path, my view is that to suggest that Weil's life is absurd or anomalous, to the extent that our lives could never approximate her own, has the effect of preventing us from dwelling with the possibility that the absurd actions Weil performed *in fact follow from* her understanding of the injustices she was implicated in given that she was living in a capitalist empire. Thought this way, her absurd actions become re-understood as radical ones. In regard to the tendency to pathologize, I wonder whether scholars trained in the humanities are qualified to make such diagnostic claims. Further, it says something about our society when we pathologize someone who, on their own terms, was seeking justice. For these reasons, when I reference Weil's biography in this book, I do so to argue that Weil consistently listened to parts of French society that were in the process of transformation: she sought out the gaps and fragments in collective life that called forth a new future, one of fair labor (not yet in the factory, but seen in fleeting moments) and international solidarity (not yet the order of Europe, but seen in the Spanish Civil War). I argue that Weil practiced a "true" philosophy not because she got the world correct—that is, that she made claims that could be empirically verified like the color of a wall—but because she tried to think in and through the world.[32]

* * *

Commenting on Weil's well-known line on friendship in a letter to her friend—"Let us love this distance, which is thoroughly woven with friendship, since those of us who do not love each other are not separated"—writer Rebecca Solnit notes that "when that friend arrives on the doorstep, something remains impossibly remote: when you step forward to embrace them your arms are wrapped around mystery, around the unknowable, around that which cannot be possessed. The far seeps even to the nearest. After all we hardly know our own depths."[33] With Stonebridge, I have already noted that in this book I present Weil as a thinker in and of her world (as a corrective to reading her as a near totally detached mystic seeking withdrawal). With Bourgault, I have started to suggest that Weil is a complex thinker of politics, including relationships of care (as a corrective to reading her as a saint or to focus on her sexuality). With Solnit, I aim to return to Weil some of her own depths. The Weil I have in mind is, as singer Patti Smith puts it in reading Weil, "an admirable model for a multitude of mindsets."[34]

Perhaps even sympathetic readers will argue that I have gone too far in my generous reading, or misreading, of Weil—Weil more as a multitudinous thinker of plurality, as a political philosopher who cultivated a negative capability and a deep engagement with others and the world, and less as a mad woman, saint, or genius who sought primarily to transcend what ties her to the world here and now. Cross-dressing and spending all her time among the poor, they will say—of course she was crazy! My response is twofold. First, my aim is not so much to read Weil "correctly," in a diagnostic sense, as it is to suggest new angles through which we can study her contributions to theory and practice. Second, and to reiterate, one of the strengths of Western philosophy is that the tradition is sufficiently varied to include under the heading of "philosopher" someone condemned and abjected for her original views, for literally standing with the oppressed, for cross-dressing, and so on. As part of a thought experiment or an exercise in thinking, I want to ask again: What if she was not mentally ill? What if she was a philosopher living out her commitments to justice?

Chapter Outline

In chapter 1 I argue that Weil's method is the essay, not just as a form of writing but as a mode of testing (or "essaying") her ideas against the material conditions of the world. I first read her 1934 essay "Reflections Concerning the Causes of Liberty and Social Oppression." I then read her "Factory Journal" (1934–1935), which records how she tested her theories from "Reflections" by placing herself in French factories. I conclude by stating the fruits of Weil's method for political philosophy today: an interrogation of present political keywords ("resistance" and "resilience") and a practice of philosophy as a way of life. In the late 1930s, Weil would turn her critical faculties toward another form of oppression: colonialism.

Chapter 2 focuses on Weil's critique of colonialism. While Weil had felt ashamed of France since 1930, when she read an exposé of the Yen Bay massacre in the *Petit Parisien*, she did not focus on colonialism until around 1937. This chapter examines Weil's late-1930s essays on colonialism, placing them in conversation with contemporary postcolonial and decolonial theory. I first present philosopher Judith Butler's concept of the "frame" to suggest that Weil elucidates "the colonial frame"—the way the ideology of colonialism conditions its subjects to see themselves, others, and the world in such a manner that colonial violence is normalized, legitimized, and maintained. Second, I argue that Weil reveals the colonial frame in interwar France by performing a "critical phenomenology" of colonizing society, bringing our attention to the particular, material, and everyday situations in which the ideology of colonialism manifests itself, such as instances of grieving.

The chapter concludes by offering cautionary notes against three potential responses to the colonial frame—inclusion, pity, and tolerance—and by contending that the political value of Weil's anti-colonialism lies in its emphasis on self-critique. But any claim to self-critique raises another question: How is "the self" understood?

In chapter 3, I read Weil's 1941—but published in 1944—essay "Literature and Morals" as well as her 1941—but published in 1951—essay "The Responsibilities of Literature." I take her call at the end of "The Responsibilities of Literature" for silent spiritual reflection as a jumping-off point to place her in dialogue with the artist Mark Rothko's abstract expressionism. While Weil might not have considered Rothko's paintings to be works of "genius" that could reorient the polis, I argue that the spirit of contemplation Rothko invites resonates with Weil's critique of advertising in "Literature and Morals." What Weil and Rothko offer, when taken together, is an alternative to the facile neoliberal call to reject dark nights of the soul for the sake of self-development, a call that remains obsessed with resilience that overcomes social barriers. I argue that Weil's contribution to contemporary debates on neoliberalism is found in her portrait of a self that tarries with the existential difficulties of finitude, pain, and solitude. At this point in the book, the reader might ask: Does Weil make any contributions to critiques of neoliberalism today beyond her understanding of the self? In the next chapter, I argue that she does as she turned her critical attention once again, this time toward the rising tide of rights discourse.

In chapter 4, I read Weil's 1942/1943 essay known most widely in English as "Human Personality" (*La Personne et le sacré*), outlining her critique of human rights and demonstrating how her critique prefigures many contemporary responses to the neoliberal turn in human rights. In doing so, I place her critiques of Personalism and of human rights discourse in dialogue with historian Samuel Moyn and philosopher Jessica Whyte, both of whom interrogate today's rights discourse that is comfortably entwined with neoliberal capitalism. Following political scientist Helen Kinsella's claim that Weil understands rights as a kind of political "illusion," I ultimately argue that what Weil's critique misses, in its thoroughgoing condemnation of rights, is what Hannah Arendt refuses to relinquish, namely, the perplexities of human rights.[35] For Weil's critique of human rights to be most productive, I conclude, it needs to maintain an opening for how rights claims can be deployed strategically even in our creaturely, decidedly imperfect, neoliberal moment. Given her critique of the language of rights, we might still wonder: For Weil, through what language should we make political demands?

In chapter 5, I suggest a continuity between Weil's early (and more obvious) Marxism and her later work. This chapter recognizes that Weil's critical impulse takes a different form in the final year of her life. In addition to offering critiques (of progress, of greatness, and of so-called civilization), she also sought to construct a new way of life for France as part of its rebuilding after the war. Considering her proposal for this collective reconstruction is especially important following the uprisings of 2020, which faced—and, at the time of writing this book, in many places still face—a militarized, counterrevolutionary response. In other words, the question of how to rebuild our communities—in all their political richness and spiritual depth—remains very much on many of our minds as police and military forces continue to occupy our cities. To conclude the chapter, I place Weil in dialogue with contemporary Marxists Jodi Dean and Adolph Reed Jr., thus situating her in a Marxist tradition wary of identity-based claims and in search of a wider movement.

This book will be successful if it achieves two results: if on a narrow or scholarly level, Weil scholars of my generation take up the book's invitation to engage more robustly with Weil's political writings from the 1930s; and if on a wider or cultural level, the book continues a conversation about what it means to live a life of ethical and political commitment when one is born into capitalism and empire.

NOTES

1. Francine du Plessix Gray, *Simone Weil* (New York: Penguin, 2001), 19.

2. Maurice Blanchot, "Affirmation (desire, affliction)," in *The Infinite Conversation*, trans. Susan Hanson (Minneapolis: University of Minnesota Press, 1993), 106.

3. Emmanuel Levinas, "Simone Weil against the Bible," in *Difficult Freedom: Essays on Judaism*, trans. Seán Hand (Baltimore: Johns Hopkins University Press, 1990), 133.

4. Quoted in Robert Zaretsky, "What We Owe to Others: Simone Weil's Radical Reminder" in *New York Times*, February 20, 2018, https://www.nytimes.com/2018/02/20/opinion/simone-weil-human-rights-obligations.html.

5. J. M. Perrin and Gustave Thibon, *Simone Weil as We Knew Her*, trans. Emma Craufurd (New York: Routledge, 1953), 120.

6. See Jean-François Lyotard, *Why Philosophize?*, trans. Andrew Brown (Cambridge, MA: Polity, 2013).

7. Hannah Arendt, *The Human Condition* (Chicago: University of Chicago Press, 2018), 131, n. 83.

8. See Giorgio Agamben, "Preface," in Simone Weil, *La personne et le sacré* (Paris: Rivages, 2017). Translation mine.

9. See Paul Elie, *The Life You Save May Be Your Own* (New York: Farrar, Straus and Giroux, 2003), 272, 508.

10. Susan Sontag, "Simone Weil," *New York Review of Books*, February 1, 1963, https://www.nybooks.com/articles/1963/02/01/simone-weil/.

11. Martin Andic, "Introduction," in Henry Leroy Finch, *Simone Weil and the Intellect of Grace* (New York: Continuum, 2001), 1.

12. Robert Chenavier, *Simone Weil: Attention to the Real*, trans. Bernard E. Doering (Notre Dame, IN: University of Notre Dame Press, 2012), 1.

13. Ibid., 5. It is worth noting that Chenavier's *Simone Weil. Une philosophie du travail* treats the tensions in Weil's thought. Perhaps my examples of portraits of Weil move too quickly in this introduction. My intention is to point out tendencies and implications of those portraits, not, of course, to condemn the important and longstanding work of commentators on Weil.

14. Mary Dietz, *Between the Human and the Divine: The Political Thought of Simone Weil* (Totowa, NJ: Rowman & Littlefield, 1988), xiv.

15. Ibid.

16. Lissa McCullough, *The Religious Philosophy of Simone Weil: An Introduction* (London: I.B. Tauris, 2014), 11.

17. Deborah Nelson, *Tough Enough: Arbus, Arendt, Didion, McCarthy, Sontag, Weil* (Chicago: University of Chicago Press, 2017), 9.

18. Sophie Bourgault, "Beyond the Saint and the Red Virgin: Simone Weil as Feminist Theorist of Care," *Frontiers* 35, no. 2 (2014): 1–27.

19. Dietz, *Between*, xiv.

20. See Lewis R. Gordon, *Fear of Black Consciousness* (New York: Farrar, Straus and Giroux, 2022), 65, 223.

21. Vincent Lloyd, *The Problem with Grace: Reconfiguring Political Theology* (Stanford: Stanford University Press, 2011), 137.

22. Ibid.

23. Jacqueline Rose, "An Endless Seeing," *New York Review of Books*, January 13, 2022.

24. Lyndsey Stonebridge, *Placeless People: Writing, Rights, and Refugees* (New York: Oxford University Press, 2018), 96.

25. Pierre Hadot, *Philosophy as a Way of Life: Spiritual Exercises from Socrates to Foucault*, trans. Michael Chase (Malden, MA: Blackwell, 1995), 56–58.

26. Nikolas Kompridis, *Critique and Disclosure: Critical Theory between Past and Future* (Cambridge, MA: MIT Press, 2006), 5.

27. James Tully, "Political Theory as a Critical Activity," *Political Theory* 30, no. 4 (2002): 551.

28. For a commentary on Weil's terrible prayer, as well as for an illuminating discussion of an ethical theory in Weil, see Yoon Sook Cha, *Decreation and the Ethical Bind: Simone Weil and the Claim of the Other* (New York: Fordham University Press, 2017), 8, 15.

29. But here I contradict myself, because in my first chapter I will rely on her "Factory Journal," itself a kind of notebook, and one certainly not meant for publication in the way some of her other essays were. While I do not judge Weil's mental health based on my reading of this journal, I do draw some philosophical and conceptual conclusions from it. Is that to say I think there is a substantial distinction between her factory journal and her notebooks? Certainly not. I simply felt that I needed to engage it in order to see how she reflected on her practical test of her 1930s theoretical

writings on labor, solidarity, and the possibility of revolution. Perhaps other scholars have felt a similar need to engage her notebooks.

30. Keats himself came up with this phrase in a letter to his brothers. He defined negative capability in striking, if gendered, terms as "when a man is capable of being in uncertainties, Mysteries, doubts, without any irritable reaching after fact & reason." For this quotation as well as extensive commentary on the phrase, see Brian Rejack and Michael Theune, eds., *Keats's Negative Capability: New Origins and Afterlives* (Liverpool: Liverpool University Press, 2019), xviii–xix.

31. Blanchot, *Infinite Conversation*, 106.

32. For this sense of a "true" philosophy, see Lyotard, *Why Philosophize?*, 106.

33. Rebecca Solnit, *A Field Guide to Getting Lost* (New York: Penguin, 2005), 29. For a translation of Weil's letter to Thibon, see *Simone Weil as We Knew Her*, 124.

34. Patti Smith, *Devotion* (New Haven, CT: Yale University Press, 2017), 9.

35. See Helen M. Kinsella, "Of Colonialism and Corpses: Simone Weil on Force," in *Women's International Thought: A New History*, eds. Patricia Owens and Katharina Rietzler (Cambridge: Cambridge University Press, 2021), 72–92.

Chapter 1

Critique of Revolution

In this chapter, I read a selection of Simone Weil's political philosophy in the way that she reads Marx—as forming "not a doctrine but a method of understanding and action" (OL 44/47). My view is that Weil's method is likewise twofold: she attempts to understand the world through inquiry, and then she tests her understanding through action. First, I read "Reflections Concerning the Causes of Liberty and Social Oppression" (1934). In that essay, inquiry, exemplified by Weil's calling into question the term "revolution," is her way of understanding reality around her, including forces of oppression and possibilities for liberation. Second, I read her "Factory Journal" (1934–1935), which records how she tested her theories from "Reflections" by placing herself in French factories. I conclude by stating the fruits of Weil's method for political philosophy today: an interrogation of political keywords (e.g., resistance, resilience) and a practice of philosophy as a way of life.[1]

From her early writings onward, Weil concerned herself with questions of philosophical method. Her dissertation, "Science and Perception in Descartes," criticizes modern science for its elevation of abstraction over and against perception and intuition. She needed to read across Descartes's *oeuvre* in order to present her contrarian point, namely, that Descartes endorsed ordinary perception as a function of understanding. This epistemological reading of Descartes carried political implications. In effect, Weil claims, the hierarchy of abstraction over perception maintains science as the prerogative of elites, because, on this account, "reasoning in common people is closely tied to intuition" but not to knowledge *per se* (FW 34/SS 12). In her study of Descartes, Weil concludes that there is "a common wisdom" that is "much closer to authentic philosophy than is the kind of thinking that study produces"; indeed, "[p]erception itself . . . is of the same nature as science," itself a mode of reasoning (FW 53/SS 32, 33).

Weil's reading of Descartes thus rescues from modern science quotidian practices as modes of knowledge production.[2] Ordinary, daily work—such as baking bread or planting trees—provides a point of entry for knowledge. Her reading also offers a more authentic *scientia*, a wisdom not of abstraction but of orientation or direction. For her, science "is not at all a matter of thinking conveniently but of thinking well, that is, by directing one's thought properly" (FW 45/SS 23). Proper direction is toward causes. She quotes Descartes to make her point: "Analysis shows the real way a thing was methodically discovered, and shows how effects depend on causes"; this analysis is different from synthesis, which "does not teach the method by which the thing was discovered" (FW 45, 46/SS 24). More than just solving a problem, analysis involves understanding how something became problematic in the first place. A focus on causes and not effects was a key insight Weil learned from Descartes. Thinking rigorously involves analysis that starts from causes. Weil would hold on to this methodological principle in her early political writings.

A POLITICAL EPISTEMOLOGY

Original and heterodox in her own analysis, Weil was constantly frustrated by the conventional political theory of her day, which posed "political and juridical transformation" as capable of abolishing capitalist oppression (OL 40/43). For her, this political theory was limited in that it began from effects. Reading Marx through Descartes in response, Weil claims that to begin from the actual causes means starting from "the very foundations of our social life," namely, the specific division of labor that resulted from the separation of manual and intellectual labor (OL 40/43). This separation is the foundation of modern culture, "a culture of specialists" (OL 40/44). In turn, she calls not merely for a shift in intellectual training, but for a redefinition of what counts as science and as a valuable knowledge practice. "Science is a monopoly," she writes, "not because public education is badly organized, but by its very nature; non-scientists have access only to the results, not to the methods, that is to say that they can only believe, not assimilate" (OL 40/44). A factory worker pulls a lever; he gets results without method, without necessarily understanding how the machine works. "And the same applies," Weil continues, "on the political plane" (OL 40/44). State bureaucracy, military, and police, in their functional separation from the population, echo the distinction found in the factory: "the managerial and executive functions" remain separate (OL 41/44). But Weil locates the cause of oppression differently from Marx. On her analysis, capitalist society does not carry within it the conditions for "real democracy"; rather, "the establishment of such a régime presupposes a preliminary transformation in the realm of production and that of culture" (OL 41/44). *And that of culture.* That is, without the abolition of the specialist culture—the "radical distinction" between managers and executors, knowers and doers—so-called revolution would only perpetuate oppression (OL 41/44). It would be a change only in ownership of production. It would, that is, be a change of the consequences and not of the causes. This was Weil's insight. This is why analysis is key. At stake in method is liberty itself.

In what follows, I read Weil's method as I think she herself did: not as a professional approach to texts but as a way of engaging the world. This reading recalls the Greek root of *method, ὁδός*, meaning "way." What Weil's method ultimately gives us is a kind of *hodos biou*, a way of life. Reading what she called her first "magnum opus,"[3] the 1934 "Reflections Concerning the Causes of Liberty and Social Oppression," I argue that Weil's philosophical method consists in understanding the world through inquiry, a mode of questioning. But Weil never rested content with asking questions. She also strove to essay her ideas in the world as well as on the page. To account for her turn to practice, I then read her "Factory Journal" to present her way of testing her theories articulated in "Reflections." My conclusion will suggest a few ways that we can learn from Weil's method today—next steps on the path she outlines. Indeed, her critique of revolution resonates for political actors calling into question the political keywords of our own time.

UNDERSTANDING: INQUIRY AND TERMINOLOGY

"The present period is one of those when everything that seems normally to constitute a reason for living dwindles away, when one must on pain of sinking into confusion or apathy [*le désarroi ou l'inconscience*], call everything into question again" (OL 36/40). So Simone Weil begins her 1934 essay "Reflections Concerning the Causes of Liberty and Social Oppression." And so does the present seem, to a number of us, to be a time of despair, confusion, and pessimism. Weil responds with the suggestion of *inquiry*, the art both of asking precise questions and of calling into question the forces at play and the powers that be in one's present. Thus, she follows two of her early and lasting influences—Socrates in his formations of questions and Descartes in his radical doubt. That precise inquiry promises a clarity of analysis such that one avoids "sinking into confusion" is itself clear. But Weil suggests that questioning does more than avoid confusion. It is also a way to avoid sinking into *l'inconscience*—not so much apathy as thoughtlessness or unthinking. By linking thoughts to potential actions, questioning is how one moves from sinking to swimming strongly, even if against the current.

What a general strike is to the workers' strike of a specific factory, Weil's inquiry is to raising questions about a single sphere of life under capitalism and the State.[4] To return to the opening line of "Reflections": when *everything* falls to pieces [*tout . . . s'évanouit*], *everything* must be called into question [*l'on doit . . . tout remettre en question*]. This is why, after a second sentence on the spread of authoritarianism and nationalism as well as the depth of these evils, she poses to herself the question of whether or not there exists a sphere of life not "poisoned" by present conditions (OL 36/40). She details the spheres—work, political leadership, technics, science, art, and family—to conclude that, alas, no such nontoxic sphere exists. Hence the present is overall not hopeful but *angoissant*—anguished, anxious, distressed.

The second aspect that forms Weil's inquiry, the art of calling into question, often takes as its focus something more specific than production or spheres of life, namely, the words themselves used to describe such phenomena. Weil's method includes a precise focus on how words are defined, employed, and consequential—what she would later call "the power of words" (cf. SWA 238–58). We might refer to this focus as Weil's concern for terminology. Having understood her point that the anxious present is poisoned in all spheres of life, we expect Weil to provide a kind of antidote. "However," she begins her second paragraph disjunctively, "ever since 1789, there has been one magic word which contains within itself all imaginable futures, and is never so full of hope as in desperate situations—that word is revolution" (OL 37/41). "Revolution" is a "magic word" because it lacks material grounding; it invokes the impossible without a relation to what is (physically and politically) feasible. "Revolution," as "the sudden reversal of the relationship between forces," she writes, defining the term as part of inquiring into it, "is not only a phenomenon unknown in history, but furthermore, if we examine it closely, something literally inconceivable, for it would be a victory of weakness over force, the equivalent of a balance whose lighter scale were to go down" (OL 74/75). In arguing this way, Weil disappoints, observing clearly that what the Left in her time took as an antidote was in fact a placebo. "Revolution" is a word in which one places one's hopes, but which lacks "anything rigorous" and, moreover, "is conjured up for demagogic purposes by apprentice dictators" (OL 38/42). Hence Weil calls the term into question.

Questioning is the "first duty" that "the present period imposes on us" (OL 38/42). That is, the present conditions press on us—and here Weil shifts from one's asking oneself to a "we," some collective or public—"to ask ourselves if the term 'revolution' is anything else but a name, if it has any precise content, if it is not simply one of the lies produced by the capitalist system in its rise to power which the present crisis is doing us the service of dissipating" (OL 38/42). This is a difficult question to ask, she acknowledges, for many have sacrificed their lives for this word. But this difficulty also signals importance. If the word is empty or if it is, indeed, promulgated as necessary friction for the capitalist ascent to power—ultimately cut through as easily as a commercial or military jet uses the wind against it in order to take flight—then "revolution" is a term with much at stake, deserving theoretical consideration and critique.

Again Weil answers her own question. The painful truth is that "revolution" is an empty term—"a word for which you kill, for which you die, for which you send the laboring masses to their death, but which does not possess any content" (OL 53/56). She does not, however, simply abandon the term. The problem of content is part of a problem of definition: the contestations around "revolution" as a term "can only be smoothed over by the most ambiguous formula"; and in addition to its lack of clarity, many invoke it, but "there are perhaps not two who attach the same content to the term" (OL 53/56). Again prefiguring her later claims about the power of words, these lines suggest terminological clarification and consistency as a way of saving lives. "Revolution," a word with immense social traction in her day and especially in her Marxian *milieu*, need not be given up, she concludes. But it must be explained with a shared or communal content if it is to carry promising political meaning.

"[P]erhaps one can give a meaning [*un sens*] to the revolutionary ideal, if not as a possible prospect in view, at any rate as a theoretical limit of feasible social transformations [*limite théorique des transformations sociales réalisables*]" (OL 53/56). With the invocation of *réalisable*, Weil is working between possibility and impossibility. We cannot, at present, see ahead to a coming revolution. And there are no guarantees. In this context, Weil focuses on an ideal as a maximum of what can be achieved, that is, what can be rendered possible or real. Here she is also making a point more specific than condemning oppressed people for dreaming of liberty. In fact, she describes such dreams both as an anthropological given—the fact that the human is a "thinking creature" means that each dreams of liberty—and as a part of the "permanent revolt" of the oppressed (OL 79, 66/80, 68). Her more specific point is that a dream is not a method. When dreaming of liberty is taken as a method, it serves as "an opium" (OL 79/80). In this way, dreaming can both motivate and prevent *realizing* liberty. For her, the first actual step toward liberty is conceptualizing it.

Weil presents conceptualizing liberty as idealizing it. "One can only steer towards an ideal. The ideal is just as unattainable [*irréalisable*] as the dream, but differs from the dream in that in concerns reality" (OL 79–80/80). She continues by adding to feasibility both calculation and hierarchy, such that the ideal "enables one, as a mathematical limit, to grade situations, whether real or realizable [*ou réelles ou réalisables*], in an order of value from least to greatest" (OL 80/80–81). Whether real or realizable, meaning that the ideal serves as a standard against which to judge not only what is occurring at present but also what could be made possible, that is, what can be realized. Importantly, what is left out of her application of the ideal is the unrealizable or impossible. To contemporary ears this exclusion might sound strange. Perhaps, one thinks, it makes sense to use an ideal to compare equally unrealizable or unfeasible alternatives ("dreams," in Weil's language), such as when theorists at academic conferences, with no apparent connection to organizing on the Left, read Marx for "openings" onto a liberty "to come." This is not how Weil reads Marx. Any lack of connection to concrete actions is a practice she condemns as "developed passivity, neglect, the habit of expecting everything from the outside, the belief in miracles" (OL 110/109). I will return to this point in this book's conclusion.

She allows for a more instrumental role for the ideal, invested not in a future to come but in what is realizable in present situations through *praxis*. The ideal she employs corrects the modern misdefinition of liberty: her claim is that true liberty is a unity not of desire and satisfaction but of thought and action (OL 81/82). Using this definition of liberty to judge societies, she sees clearly that modern industrial society is unfree, because it relies on increasing specialization through which a knowledgeable managerial class is separated from a functional working class. Indeed, modern civilization is completely unbalanced: humans become little more than cogs as the State takes a central role in economic and social life, subordinating citizens' interests to its military expansion. A further irony and reversal: in modern life, collectivities, such as political parties and trade unions, crush individuality by reproducing what they claim to abolish. Both bureaucracy in politics and mechanization in industry further separate thought and action. To read Weil's ideal as a tool for evaluation is to say that she is concerned with axiology—philosophical inquiry pertaining to value (ethics and aesthetics).

We can see how Weil's discussion of a toxic modern culture and, in response, her sketch of an ideal to move toward, align with ethics in both the descriptive and etymological *ethos* and the prescriptive, teleological "ethical." It is harder to understand what she is doing in regard to aesthetics. But aesthetics, I submit, is a central concern in her essay, integral to her method both when "aesthetics" is understood in a narrow, technical sense (as art) and in a broad, etymological sense (related to feeling). In her long opening paragraph, she specified art as one sphere of life poisoned by capitalism and the State: the "general confusion" of modern life, with its split between abstract knowledge and concrete action—for Weil it is a tragedy that the machinist in the factory usually does not know how to make her product, just how to pull the levers—"partly deprives [art] of its public, and by that fact impairs inspiration" (OL 37/41). Further, the question of the revolutionary ideal, as we saw above, is one of giving it *un sens*, where that term can be heard as both direction and sense, orientation and feeling. In this way, part of the task of providing content to "revolution" is guiding the senses.

For Weil, providing content to political keywords involves engaging with their political implications. How, on her analysis, do oppression and responses to it function? And how is this political question related to aesthetics? "The powerful, be they priests, military leaders, kings or capitalists," she writes, "always believe that they command by divine right; and those who are under them feel themselves crushed [*se sentent écrasés*] by a power which seems to them either divine or diabolical, but in any case supernatural" (OL 69/71). Oppression here is a certain feeling, and "times of popular agitation occur," Weil claims, when both "rebellious slaves and threatened masters . . . forget how heavy and solid the chains of oppression are" (OL 69/71). Oppression has weight and density. It is felt, and it is a kind of limitation on feeling—oppression is a kind of anesthetization. Finally, amidst "this religion of power," "each one thinks that power resides mysteriously in one of the classes to which he has no access, because hardly anybody understands that it resides nowhere" (OL 111/109). For Weil there is no power *per se*—only a struggle for power taken as the goal or end when, in fact, it is a means. The irony is that, as modern humans have freed themselves from some constraints of nature, we have enslaved ourselves to the whims of power struggles. What results is "that dizzy fear which is always brought about by loss of contact with reality" (OL 111/110). In the context of anguish and anxiety, the dominant feeling is fear. That Weil emphasizes the sense of fear as predominant in modern society should not be lost on our considerations of her method.

Thus far I have presented Weil's method in terms of inquiry—in general as a way of calling into question and, in particular, as a way to question how words are used and what they mean. I have underscored the importance of both idealization and aesthetics for her method. I will now transition from *inquiry*, the basis of Weil's method of understanding the reality around her, to *essaying*, the basis of Weil's method of action.

ACTION: ESSAYING REALITY

In making explicit Weil's method, I would be remiss if my focus remained only on her method of understanding as exemplified in "Reflections," what she called her "inventory of modern civilization [*l'inventaire de la civilisation présente*]" (OL 116/114). Weil's is a method not just of understanding but also of action. Having written "Reflections," she applied for a sabbatical from teaching on June 20, 1934. In her request for leave, she wrote, "I want to prepare a philosophy thesis concerning the relationship of modern technique, the basis of large industry, to the essential aspects of our civilization—that is, on the one hand, our social organization and, on the other, our culture."[5] She also referred to her projected study as her "research."[6] But she was not preparing an academic manuscript; hers would be an essay of a different kind. On and off from 1934–1935, she worked in the factories around Paris.

Weil set as the goal of her research method the understanding of her civilization in terms of its society and culture. Her method for such a "thesis" and "research" was to work amidst the jetsam of her civilization, namely, precarious workers in factories. Understanding was never enough for Weil. That is, a theoretical grasp—an inventory—of civilization remained limited without being informed by practical experience. The point was not just to inquire into the world. It was to act within it with a view toward changing it.

Because Weil's year of factory work tends to be romanticized by Weil scholars—a time of pure sacrifice and latent spiritual development—we would do well to consider its own material conditions. Trying to avoid hagiography when biography is required, in this section, I pay particular attention the historical events that shaped Weil's factory year. She rented a small room on 228 rue Lecourbe to live near her job and to do so (semi-)independently from her parents.[7] Through Boris Souvarine, editor of *La Critique Sociale*—a small Leftist journal critical of Stalinism in which Georges Bataille, among others, would publish—Weil knew Auguste Detoeuf, managing director of Alsthom Company, which produced electrical machinery for French trams and underground railways. It was from Detoeuf that Weil acquired her first factory job; lacking a work certificate, she likely would not have had access to factory labor without the help of her contacts, whom she knew because of her elite education. Like so many in Weil's life, Detoeuf saw the need to protect her in some sense, asking the factory foreman to keep an eye on her, a protection her fellow workers did not share.

On Tuesday, December 4, 1934, she began work as a power-press operator at the Alsthom Company factory. She entered the factory as part of its most oppressed group, unskilled female workers. Always writing, she kept a "Factory Journal" to note her observations. It begins with two telling epigraphs. The first is from the *Iliad* and in Greek, translated as "Much against your will, under pressure of a harsh necessity" (FW 155/CO 29). The second is from Weil herself and reads, "Not only should man know what he is making, but if possible he should see how it is used—see how nature is changed by him. Every man's work should be an *object of contemplation* for him" (FW 155/CO 29). Thus, Weil situates her factory year as living under necessity, natural and social, with a view toward a unity of knowledge and use, intellectual and manual labor. This is to say, Weil was to subject herself to oppression so as to better understand liberty.

"I'm very happy to have done this after having dreamed of it for so long," she wrote in a letter from around December 11.[8] "I think more and more that the liberation (relative) of the workers must be brought about before all else in the workshop, and it seems to me that I will manage to perceive something of what that depends on."[9] Due to the economic crisis in France at the time, Weil was temporarily laid off from Christmas to New Year's Day. On her first days back at work, January 2 and 3, 1935, in the coppersmiths' workshop, while she placed copper bobbins into and took them out of a furnace, skilled work was conducted around her. She writes of Friday, January 4, "Totally different place, although right next to our shop . . . Relaxed and brotherly atmosphere, no more servility or pettiness . . . At last, a happy workshop. Teamwork . . . Numerous calculations, needed for measurements" (FW 163/CO 37–38). There was a sense, then, that in some parts of the factory a partial union of manual and intellectual labor occurred. But Weil's delight at this exception only proved the rule. She was concerned about how education in France often remained the prerogative of the elite. One result of this classism was that factory bosses treated workers not as humans who could understand their tasks or work collaboratively but as mere laborers who functioned to pull levers and generate products. With Marx, then, Weil observed the worker's alienation from product, others, and self.

In a long entry dated Monday, January 14, 1935, she writes, "The effect of exhaustion is to make me forget my real reasons for spending time in the factory, and to make it almost impossible for me to overcome the strongest temptation that this life entails: that of not thinking anymore, which is the one and only way of not suffering from it" (FW 171/CO 45). To not suffer one must *not* think. And after this submission, thought is painful. Despair is the natural consequence. Moreover, revolt is limited circumstantially: the reality is that working without efficiency leads to starvation (FW 171/CO 45). From nearly the beginning of her time in the factories, then, we see Weil developing what would become a key observation: daily life in the modern factory is felt painfully as physical and emotional stresses of labor become incorporated.

She had awoken with ear pain on January 10. On January 15, she went to a doctor and received the diagnosis of otitis. As a result, she moved in again with her parents on rue Auguste-Comte, where she would stay for over a month. During this period of sickness, she wrote in a letter about her position among the factory workers: "My capacity for adaptation is almost unlimited, so that I am able to forget that I am a 'qualified lecturer' on tour in the working class."[10] With an inflamed ear, and now anemic, at the direction of her parents Weil then went with her mother to Montana, Switzerland, arriving February 3. Activities in Montana included skiing. With her mother, she returned to France on February 22, moving back to rue Lecourbe on Saturday, February 23, and recommencing factory work on Monday, February 25. After her first week back at work, her headaches began again. At the end of her second week back, she learned that she was to be laid off for another two weeks, from March 8 onward. During this period without work, she wrote to a friend that "since I am here [in the factory] *first of all to observe and understand*, I cannot produce this mental void inside me, this absence of thought indispensable to the slaves of modern machinery."[11] (How are we to hear this invocation of slavery? Is she too quick in using it? My sense is that, because she was, in the early 1930s, consistently engaged with Marx's writings, here she is echoing Marx's language about workers as slaves to capital.[12])

She also wrote to one of her former students from Le Puy that in the factory she had "escaped from a world of abstractions to find myself among real men" and that goodness is something real in a factory "because the least act of kindness . . . calls for a victory over fatigue and the obsession with pay . . . thought, too, calls for an almost miraculous effort of rising above the conditions of one's life."[13] She returned to work again on Monday, March 18, but she left Alsthom in early April. The last day mentioned in her Factory Journal is Tuesday, April 2. Her certificate of service from Alsthom reads December 4, 1934, to April 5, 1935. It is not clear why she left Alsthom—whether she quit or was fired remains unknown.

Looking for work in early April, when the unemployment rate was near 20 percent in France, Weil had a conversation with two metal fitters who were in search of jobs. They spent the morning—presumably Wednesday, April 10—in free conversation "on a plane above the miseries of existence that are the dominant preoccupation of slaves, especially the women" (FW 199/CO 72). Weil writes of this encounter, "Total feeling of comradeship. For the first time in my life, in short. No barrier, either in the class difference (since it is suppressed), or sexual difference. Miraculous" (FW 200/CO 72). This note reveals how Weil saw her own position during her year of factory work, namely, that she had sufficiently broken with her class such that she could truly be a comrade. But it was precisely because she had not done so that she kept working in the factories; only with her parents' financial and medical support, as well as with her connections to Detoeuf, could Weil remain a factory worker "on tour."

She restarted work on Tuesday, April 11, 1935, at the J. J. Carnaud et Forges de Basse-Indre factory at rue du Vieux Pont de Sèvres, Boulogne-Billancourt. On the first day she did not "make the rate," but the factory manager told her to come back the following day anyway.[14] Fatigued, and needing fresh air, she went to rest by the Seine. "In spite of my fatigue [*fatigue*] . . . there I sit on the bank, on a stone, gloomy, exhausted [*épuisée*], my heart gripped by impotent rage, feeling drained of all my vital substance," she wrote painfully, continuing, "I wonder if, in the event that I were condemned to live this life, I would be able to cross the Seine every day without someday throwing myself in" (FW 201/CO 73). On April 21, Easter Sunday, in an effort that would become her holiday tradition, she went to a Catholic church with the hope of hearing Gregorian chant, but was disappointed. She was then fired from the second factory on May 7, 1935. Upon asking the foreman why she had been fired, he said, "I don't have to account to you for anything."[15] Weil's journal, blank for the four weeks she spent at the Carnaud factory, suggests that this was the most difficult period for her during her factory year.

She then traveled to a number of other factories in an attempt to find another job. Limiting herself to a daily budget of three francs and fifty centimes in good ethnographic fashion, by the third week of looking for a job, she writes, "Hunger becomes a permanent feeling"—more painful than working.[16] On May 31 she applied to the Ministry of Education for a position teaching philosophy during the next academic year, preferably one near Paris. Because of this application, Weil knew that her next factory position would likely be her last. On Wednesday, June 5, after putting on her friend Simone Pétrement's makeup to look attractive to the man in charge of hiring, Weil secured a job at the Renault plant, where she would work the 2:30–10:00 pm shift running not the presses, as she deeply feared, but a milling machine. On Thursday, June 6, she writes, "The disadvantage of being in the position of a slave is that you are tempted to think that human beings who are pale shadows in the cave really exist" (FW 206/CO 78). Her reference to Plato's *Republic* is indicative of both the impossibility of thinking in the midst of factory work and the need, which she experienced firsthand, for reorienting the French polity. At this time slavery was becoming a more important theme in her journal. On the morning of Thursday, June 27, she had strange reaction to boarding the W bus.

> How is it that I, a slave [*moi, l'esclave*], can get on this bus and ride on it for my 12 sous just like anyone else? . . . If someone brutally ordered me to get off, telling me that such comfortable forms of transportation are not for me . . . I think that would seem completely natural to me. Slavery has made me entirely lose the feeling of having any rights. It appears to me a favor when I have a few moments in which I have nothing to bear in the way of human brutality. These moments are like smiles from heaven, a gift of chance. (FW 211/CO 82)

Her language here is telling of the shift in her thinking during the factor year. Now, merely going through the day without oppression is seen *as a favor, as supererogatory*. Beaten and fatigued by oppressive labor, she notes that making a claim to her rights has become an impossibility. In the modern factory brutality is naturalized, such that non-brutality is seen as a gift—one from out of this world, this world of slavery. Only in fleeting moments of non-brutality could reason develop. Only in the gaps of oppression could liberty be stirred. Indeed, she continues, her fellow workers, her "comrades," "haven't fully understood that they are slaves," such that the words "just" and "unjust" only carry a partial meaning for them, and insofar as they live in a situation "in which everything is injustice," their reason cannot develop (FW 211/CO 82).

Even at the "cushy job" on the factory floor, Weil struggled. Her Factory Journal is dotted with the language of fear (FW 205/CO 77). Though her Renault work certificate says June 6 to August 22, Weil's last journal entry that mentions work at Renault is on Thursday, August 8. According to Weil's friend and biographer Simone Pétrement, Weil likely finished at Renault before August 10, because on August 10–11 she attended the National Conference of the Alliance against War at Saint-Denis. In total, her "year" of factory work amounted to around 24 weeks of laboring on the floors of factories.

In another letter to a friend Weil reflected on her experience in the factories. She claimed that modern industrial slavery comprised two elements principally: the increase in pace and the orders from superiors. While the factory managers continued to demand increased speeds of production, both fatigue and thinking slowed work. Orders could occur at any time; the result is that the worker lives in constant fear and dread and, thereby, in a state of degradation. "The main fact isn't the suffering," she writes in one of the last lines of her Factory Journal, "but the humiliation" (FW 225/CO 96). Her (and others') reaction to this slavery—a slavery not only *of* the precarious economic circumstances but also contained *in* the mechanical work itself—surprised her. "[O]ppression," she concludes, "does not engender revolt as an immediate reaction, but submission [*n'engendre pas comme réaction immédiate la révolte, mais la soumission*]" (FW 226/CO 96).

Perhaps the most striking example of forced docility comes from a fellow precarious female worker, documented in Weil's January 9 entry: "A woman drill operator had a clump of hair completely torn out by her machine, despite her hairnet; a large bald patch is visible on her head. It happened at the end of the morning. She came to work in the afternoon just the same, although she was in a lot of pain and was even more afraid" (FW 166–67/CO 41). Echoing Weil's aesthetic focus in "Reflections," this documentation also recalls Weil's observation in April 1935: "In this kind of life those who suffer aren't able to complain . . . Everywhere the same callousness, like the foremen's with few exceptions" (FW 203/CO 75). Not only is there an inability to have voice under conditions of oppression, Weil observes, but the human herself must also continue working in pain as if she were an anesthetic machine. Yet, Weil continues in a letter after the year of factory work, "Slowly and painfully, in and through slavery, I reconquered the sense of my human dignity—a sense that this time relied upon nothing outside myself."[17] This is a key theme in Weil's Factory Journal, what her biographer David McLellan insightfully refers to as the dialectic of self-respect and humiliation.[18] As we have seen, in Weil's Factory Journal the latter emerged much more strongly.

In sum, through factory work Weil's political pessimism deepened. From her experiences as a worker she could write that the workers are "[t]he class of those *who do not count*—in any situation—in anyone's eyes."[19] She did not find the means for liberating the workers, as she had written as the goal of her "research" in her request for a sabbatical. In reflecting on her time in factories in early August, she asks herself what she gained from her experience. Her answer:

> The feeling that I do not possess any right whatever, of any kind (take care not to lose this feeling). The ability to be morally self-sufficient, to live in this state of constant latent humiliation without feeling humiliated in my own eyes; to savor every moment of freedom or camaraderie, as if it would last forever. A direct contact with life. (FW 225/CO 95)

In comparison with her pre-factory "Testament," we see that Weil maintains the language of liberty, but she moves from oppression to humiliation. Her method of action heightened her sense of suffering, arguably allowing for the conceptual development of what she would later call *malheur* (affliction). In other words, through working in the factory amidst others, Weil began to understand more potential dimensions of suffering. There are several paradoxes to how she gained this knowledge. It is noteworthy that she described increased contact with life and reality only after *choosing* to be ground down in surreal, mechanical environments. Her increased appreciation for liberty and solidarity occurred amidst a context of oppression and instrumentalized relations.[20] For me, Weil's time spent working in factories raises a number of questions. In particular, does her choice to work alongside the downtrodden limit her comradeship, the sense of "camaraderie" she notes in the lines above? Is it more akin to liberation theology's preferential option for the poor, or to how wealthy people today need intense cycling studios and backpacking trips to feel contact with reality? In general, what are the political promises of Weil's factory work? What can we learn from her method of action?

THE POLITICAL IMPLICATIONS OF
UNDERSTANDING AND ACTION

I have presented Weil's method as twofold, consisting in understanding and action or, more specifically, in inquiring and essaying. While I have articulated this claim by reading "Reflections" and "Factory Journal" together, I think we could extend it to much of Weil's major political writings and experiments (her other essays): from her 1932 "Capital and the Worker" followed by traveling to study trade unionism in Germany to her 1936 "Antigone" followed by attending workers' strikes in Paris to her 1937 "Let Us Not Start Another Trojan War: The Power of Words" followed by proposing a frontline nursing corps to restore the balance of the war, Weil consistently posed and responded to the most pertinent political questions of her day in theory and then attempted to test her conclusions in practice. This method itself became dialectical: it was not always a new, clean inquiry followed by actions responding only to that inquiry; rather, Weil's developing inquiries built on previous actions. I would maintain, however, that one principle of her early writings remained in her method throughout her life: to some extent, an inquiry into the causes of the political issue must be conducted rigorously *before* action is taken, lest that action lead to changes in the appearance of relations in society without shifting its fundamental organization (what Weil called its "culture").

In presenting Weil's method, I have also underscored her focus on aesthetics—the predominant feelings as well as the role of art in both oppression and liberty. The purpose of this chapter has been more analytical than practical: I have raised a question about what Weil's method is and answered my question in terms of understanding and action by reading two of her writings from 1934–1935. But we might also consider a practical note. In assuming his chair at the Collège de France in 1983, Pierre Hadot invoked the older *philosophia* instead of "philosophy," "reserv[ing] the right to follow this *philosophia* in its most varied manifestations and above all to eliminate the preconceptions the word *philosophy* may evoke in the modern mind."[21] Above I outlined Weil's method as pursuing philosophy as a way of life. One limit of this chapter is that it could function to reduce Weil's inspiring, contradictory, and multifaceted practice of philosophy—what Hadot calls "varied manifestations"—simply to the two headings of inquiry and action. To avoid this reduction, and to take a practical turn, we might consider the varying promises of Weil's method.

Weil teaches that there is always more to be questioned and especially more to be done. We can ask: As we conduct research, whom should we include in our collaborations, and whose recognition would we seek (Department Chair or student, Dean or custodian)? How might we supplement the political keyword of our time, "resistance," by attending to the aesthetics of oppression and liberty? And how might we also interrogate other predominant terms, such as the neoliberal "resilience"? Conducting this attention and interrogation is especially difficult when "[o]urs," as Rebecca Rozelle-Stone puts it, reading Weil, "is an age characterized by obsession with watching but an inability to attend," when, that is, technological distraction has become "not simply an individual intellectual problem, but also a fundamentally social/ ethical one."[22]

* * *

We can consider for a brief example debates in feminist philosophy around the dependency of political subjects and the question of resilience. Influential legal theorist Martha Fineman argues that "the state is . . . the legitimate governing entity and is tasked with a responsibility to establish and monitor social institutions and relationships that facilitate the acquisition of individual and social resilience."[23] Part of the role of social institutions, on Fineman's account, is to "provide for our future well being in the form of savings and investments."[24] "Human resources," she continues, "contribute to our individual development, allowing participation in the market, and the accumulation of material resources. Human resources are often referred to as 'human capital' and are primarily developed through systems that provide education, training, knowledge and experience."[25]

Reading Fineman's attempted critique of the neoliberal present through a call for individual and social resilience, I recall once again Weil's line from another early essay, the 1933 "Prospects": "[O]ne cannot disregard the fact that all the political currents which now affect the masses, whether they style themselves fascist, socialist, or communist, tend towards the same form of State capitalism" (OL 18/23). "It seems fairly clear that contemporary humanity tends pretty well everywhere to a totalitarian form of social organization," Weil went on in "Reflections," "that is to say, towards a system in which the state power comes to exercise sovereign sway in all spheres, even, indeed, above all, in that of thought" (OL 109/108). Weil offers at least two key insights here. First, she was one of the few thinkers in her time who was able to abstract away from her own situation in order to examine the very foundations of political life. As a result, she challenged political philosophers to look beyond the intellectual hegemony of the state. Her observation prefigures the scholarship of David Lloyd and Paul Thomas, who explain that the hegemony of the state operates today such that citizens and philosophers alike "accept the forms and precepts of the state at least to the extent that alternatives become literally and figuratively the state's unthinkable."[26]

The second insight Weil offers regards not just the state but her diagnosis of "State capitalism." Fineman exemplifies how accepting the hegemony of the state and the neoliberal language of resilience can be part of a return to the logic of capitalism, what Fineman calls "human capital." Weil invites political theorists today to decouple systems of human support and care (what Fineman refers to as education and training) from the logic and vocabulary of the market. Some contemporary feminist theory has made this point (even if not reading Weil but, in its method, resonating with Weil's critique of specific words). Overall, the language of resilience, Robin James notes, interrogating the word, in fact *recycles damage into more resources.*[27] According to this logic, "the person who has overcome is rewarded with increased human capital, status, and other forms of recognition and recompense, because, finally, and most importantly, this individual's own resilience boosts society's resilience."[28] Thus, resilience is best understood as a "neoliberal ethical and aesthetic ideal."[29] James's critique of "resilience" demonstrates, in the spirit of Weil, critical inquiry at pains to think in the present.[30]

METHOD AND COLLECTIVITY

Weil's method informs her relationship to collectivities. Through her intellectual and physical efforts, her work can be read as an extended reflection on the tensions between the individual and the collective—that is, on one's ability to maintain one's critical stance and one's recognition that *to realize* the implications of that stance, one must engage in political work with others, thus ceding some individuality given the pressures and pulls of collective life. In "Reflections," Weil essays the possibilities for freedom given the constraints of modern life. She analyzes precisely what links oppression, general and particular, to the system of production such that she can understand how oppression begins, subsists, transforms, and might be eliminated. As she saw it, modern civilization was completely out of balance. Humans were cogs in a bureaucratic machine as the State—the bureaucratic organization *par excellence*—became the center of economic and social life, subordinating true economic interests to military ones. Further, collectivities such as political parties and unions both crushed individuality and in fact reproduced what they claimed to abolish: bureaucracy, mechanization, a reversal of means and ends, and a separation of thought and action. In this early essay, then, we see that collectivities, in their given form, were for Weil on the side of oppression more often than that of liberty.

Weil's early essay, however, is not a denial of collectivity *per se*. Rather, it sharpens our focus on precisely how collectivities oppress individuals. Oppression, Weil argues, depends in part on arbitrary forces at play: "Actually, in all oppressive societies, any man, whatever his rank may be, is dependent not only on those above or below him, but above all on the very play of collective life—a blind play which alone determines the social hierarchies" (OL 91–92/91). This play is not on a small scale, as it might be in a village or a cluster of hunter-gatherers. In those cases, one can see, feel, and talk to those on whom one depends. By contrast, Weil is describing modern life, in which one has limited knowledge of and access to the person who delivers one's food by truck into the city, who sweeps the streets, who makes the decisions about infrastructure and education, and so on. In this way, modern collective life is "blind" yet determining.

But why are the determinations of modern social life part of an *oppressive* society, as opposed to being part of an efficient economic and social organization? In part, it is because, like a worker in a factory who does not understand the machine she operates, the modern individual has no knowledge of what constitutes her day-to-day life. This lack of knowledge gives a feeling of powerlessness and of dependency of the worst kind—on arbitrary powers. To put this differently, the modern problem is a problem of abstraction, where the forces that determine an individual's life are abstracted too far from the individual's life. Weil teaches that

> if there is one thing in the world which is completely abstract, wholly mysterious, inaccessible to the senses and to the mind, it is the collectivity; the individual who is a member of it cannot, it would seem, reach up to or lay hold of it by any artifice, bring his weight to bear on it by the use of any lever; with respect to it he feels himself to be something infinitely small. (OL 92/91)

Importantly, this is true of both those in positions of power and those who are dispossessed. "In a society founded on oppression," Weil goes on, "it is not only the weak but also the most powerful who are bond-slaves to the blind demands of collective life" (OL 96/95–96). This is a key observation. Social position notwithstanding, modern collective life affects all (though differentially) in both spirit and intellect. Just as a worker needs to fit the norms of ability and presentation to find a job, a President depends on the collective psychology of the masses to which he panders. Acknowledging how collective demands condition both the powerless and the powerful in modern life, Weil addresses in turn what a freer version of modern society could look like. Informed by her readings of Immanuel Kant, she begins: "Men would, it is true, be bound by collective ties, but exclusively in their capacity as men; they would never be treated by each other as things" (OL 94/94). Again we see that it is not the case that Weil in "Reflections" is against collectivities *per se*. Indeed, she endorses "collective ties" of some sort, a sort in which, following Kant, others are treated as ends and not means, what she will call "friendship" later in the essay. Thus, we see that the work she describes is far from the modern reality; one has to both know and care for others with whom one works.

Weil sees modern collectivities denying not just the knowledge the worker needs to understand a job. They also deny one's ability to think. "[I]n all spheres," Weil summarizes regarding modern social organization in general, "thought, the prerogative of the individual, is subordinated to vast mechanisms which crystallize collective life, and that is so to such an extent that we have almost lost the notion of what real thought is" (OL 104/103). Collectivities are not only unthinking, in that they are mechanical, but they also stifle thought. All value is subordinated to the service of the social machine. When a student wants to study art, she is asked, "What are you going to do with that?" This question means little more than how will her expression be integrated into state-sanctioned capitalism. By Weil's lights, any just collective would cultivate the opposite: social processes would work in favor of an individual's thinking, living, or dancing with others.

* * *

I have begun reading Weil's early essay because it calls our attention to criteria of a just collective, against which we can test other collectives. We have seen that, for early Weil, a collective is just if and only if it promotes the thinking of the individual. It must also allow the individual access to concrete knowledge of the forces at play in her life. Third, it must include the right relationship of means and end, not subordinating the individual to collective ends but fostering the development of the individual's own ends and preventing any individual from being treated as if she were simply a cog in a machine. These criteria are so radical as to be deeply inconsistent with modern, urban life.

For Weil, by 1936 a revolution would not change the system of production that was thoroughly based on passive obedience; it would simply change the hands who control the factory. She planned to return to Rosières on June 12 but instead went to Paris for the workers strikes.[31] There, although she was not optimistic about the results of the strikes, she wrote that "at least I could share the pure and profound joy that inspired my comrades in slavery."[32] Weil visited the Renault plant where she worked in 1935, and in her "The Life and Strike of Metal Workers," published a few days later, she noted, "What a joy to hear, instead of the merciless racket of the machines, music, songs, and laughter" in that factory.[33] By mid-1936 she was convinced she would not be hired by Rosières, so she had started a plan to work again at Detoeuf's plant.[34] But Weil's trajectory would shift dramatically because Spanish generals revolted against the Spanish Popular Front on July 17 and 18, 1936. She had approved of France's decision *not* to intervene in Spain on the Republic side (just as she had approved of nonintervention when Germany occupied the Rhineland, violating the Versailles Treaty, in March 1936).[35] She opposed fascism as part of a larger critique of authoritarian power. In going to war, she saw a surrender to the logic of power and prestige in fascism.[36] For Weil, the choice was between prestige and peace; prestige meant war, no matter its name, democracy or revolution (FW 258/EHP II, 29).[37]

On June 22, 1937, Léon Blum's Popular Front government resigned. Weil took this event as the signal of the death of the 1936 enthusiasm, which Blum failed to harness. Considering these events in her 1937 "Note on Social Democracy" [*Méditations sur un cadavre*], she writes:

> The material of the political art is the double perspective, ever shifting between the real conditions of social equilibrium and the movements of collective imagination. Collective imagination, whether of mass meetings or of meetings in evening dress, is never correctly related to the really decisive factors of a given social situation; it is always beside the point, or ahead of it, or behind it. (SE 152/EHP 90)

This statement comments on what we might call the epistemology of the collectivity: it cannot know the heart of a situation. Why not? It is in part because the collective imagination is moved by the pressures of others and not by the measured quality required in thinking. Indeed, the Platonic concept of the Great Beast stayed with Weil in different ways from "Reflections" onward; she was continually concerned with the (in)ability of collectivities to think. And for Weil, thinking always matters for politics because politics must move between the imaginary and the real, the movements at play and the obstacles in place.

Weil's primary worry in "Reflections" was the pain of nonthinking (*l'inconscience*) in a context of despair. Amidst this anxiety and distress (*angoisse*), where fear and humiliation are the dominant feelings and the noise of metal gears, the sound of a supervisor's yell, the feeling of your hair and flesh ripped from the machine are common sensations—in this aesthetic hell—even a day's work requires courage. Ultimately, Weil's method invites us to "the courage of despair"—to strength in the face of fear, to stubborn sensitivity, to continual questioning, to bold thinking, and to political action (FW 211/CO 83).[38] Going forward, having felt ashamed of France since 1930, when she read Louis Roubaud's exposé of the Yen Bay massacre in the *Petit Parisien*, Weil used her method of inquiry and action to offer a thoroughgoing critique of French colonialism around 1937. In this way, her critique of modernity would become a critique of modernity/coloniality.[39] It is to this critique that I turn next.

NOTES

1. This chapter is derived in part from an article published in *Comparative and Continental Philosophy*, November 23, 2021, copyright Taylor & Francis, available online https://www.tandfonline.com/doi/full/10.1080/17570638.2021.2002644. See

Benjamin P. Davis, "Simone Weil's Method: Essaying Reality through Inquiry and Action," *Comparative and Continental Philosophy* 13, no. 3 (2021): 1–12.

2. Lissa McCullough explains: Weil's "is an intellectually democratic ambition to illustrate that all ordinary people, however ignorant of scientific thought they may be, already employ the most fundamental and essential principles of science in their ordinary perception and daily work without being aware of it" (Lissa McCullough, "Simone Weil's Phenomenology of the Body," *Comparative and Continental Philosophy* 4, no. 2 [2012]: 197).

3. See Simone Pétrement, *Simone Weil: A Life* (New York: Pantheon, 1978), 204.

4. Weil capitalized "State" in her writings. I follow her usage.

5. See Pétrement, *Simone Weil*, 205.

6. "Research" is the same term Weil would use to refer to her project of forming a frontline nursing corps, which she developed around 1940. See Joan Dargan, *Simone Weil: Thinking Poetically* (Albany: State University of New York Press, 1999), 115.

7. Pétrement, *Simone Weil*, 225.

8. Ibid., 227.

9. Ibid.

10. Ibid., 232.

11. Ibid., 235.

12. See e.g., Karl Marx, "Relation of Wage-Labour to Capital," in *Wage Labour and Capital*, https://www.marxists.org/archive/marx/works/1847/wage-labour/index.htm.

13. Pétrement, *Simone Weil*, 235–236.

14. Ibid., 238.

15. Ibid., 239.

16. Ibid.

17. Ibid. For her time in the factory, see also ibid., 243.

18. David McLellan, *Utopian Pessimist: The Life and Thought of Simone Weil* (New York: Poseidon, 1990), 104. I rely on Pétrement and McLellan for all of my biographical context in this book. I am grateful and indebted to both of them. All errors remain my own.

19. Pétrement, *Simone Weil*, 245.

20. Scott Ritner extends this point into Weil's late work: "What Weil seems to be gambling on is—and she shares this with the Marxian tradition—the development of mass solidarity through shared hardship . . . What Marx calls class-consciousness, and Lukács demands be abolished in the act of revolution, is translated by [late] Weil into a mystical terminology of affliction, attention, decreation, and grace" (Scott B. Ritner, "Simone Weil's Heterodox Marxism: Revolutionary Pessimism and the Politics of Resistance," in *Simone Weil, Beyond Ideology?*, eds. Sophie Bourgault and Julie Daigle [London: Palgrave Macmillan, 2020], 200–201).

21. Hadot, *Philosophy as a Way of Life*, 53.

22. A. Rebecca Rozelle-Stone, "*Le Déracinement* of Attention: Simone Weil on the Institutionalization of Distractedness," *Philosophy Today* 53, no. 1 (2009): 100.

23. Martha Fineman, "Vulnerability and Inevitable Inequality," *Oslo Law Review* 4, no. 3 (2017): 134.

24. Ibid., 146.

25. Ibid.

26. David Lloyd and Paul Thomas, *Culture and the State* (New York: Routledge, 1998), 21.

27. Robin James, *Resilience & Melancholy: Pop Music, Feminism, Neoliberalism* (Alresford, UK: Zero Books, 2016), 7.

28. Ibid.

29. Ibid., 6.

30. For an extended discussion of this debate, see Benjamin P. Davis and Eric Aldieri, "Precarity and Resistance: A Critique of Martha Fineman's Vulnerability Theory," *Hypatia* 36, no. 2 (2021): 321–37.

31. Pétrement, *Simone Weil*, 263. The strikes followed the elections of April 26 and May 3, 1936; the Popular Front, formed under Léon Blum in response to growing fascism, was victorious. By the beginning of June all the large metallurgical factories in Paris were on strike through a new form, namely, the sit-in strike, the takeover of the factory. See McLellan, *Utopian Pessimist*, 114. See also Yoon Sook Cha, *Decreation and the Ethical Bind: Simone Weil and the Claim of the Other* (New York: Fordham University Press, 2017), 185, n. 78.

32. Pétrement, *Simone Weil*, 264.

33. Ibid., 265.

34. Ibid.

35. McLellan, *Utopian Pessimist*, 119.

36. Ibid., 124.

37. Jane Doering writes, "Weil warned that prestige was illusory and limitless; no nation or people had enough or was sure of keeping any imagined glory" (E. Jane Doering, *Simone Weil and the Spectre of Self-Perpetuating Force* [Notre Dame: University of Notre Dame Press, 2010], 27).

38. Cf. Pétrement, *Simone Weil*, 242.

39. I am using the slash made famous by Quijano in order to suggest that Weil's critique of colonization, following from her critique of modern social life, means that she was one of the first European philosophers to self-critically see the constitutive link described as modernity/coloniality. See Aníbal Quijano, "Coloniality of Power, Eurocentrism and Latin America," *Nepantla: Views from the South* 1, no. 3 (2000): 533–80.

Chapter 2

Critique of Colonialism

In condemning the contradictory practices of interwar France, Simone Weil criticized the self-proclaimed defender of the rights of man for favoring its population at home while oppressing others abroad. She was thus critical of the colonial ideology emerging from her country, and in doing so she was one of the first European philosophers to make explicit an anti-colonial self-critique.[1] In this chapter, I engage Weil's writings on colonialism, reading them with a focus on emotion or affect.[2] This focus will allow us to inquire into two of her most poignant observations regarding colonial society: first, that the French bourgeoisie and working classes, as well as the French Left, might shed a tear at the sight of a local beggar, but fail to cry over France's systematic destruction of people in its colonies; and second, that the French are quick to discount the tears of foreigners, those at a distance. For citizens of the colonizing nation, only certain, familiar tears count as real affliction (SWC 41–44/EHP II, 97–99).[3]

This chapter proceeds as follows: first I present philosopher Judith Butler's concept of the "frame" in order to suggest that Weil diagnoses what I call "the colonial frame," or the way in which the ideology of colonialism conditions its subjects to see themselves, others, and the world such that colonial violence is naturalized, legitimized, and maintained. I then suggest that Weil unveils the colonial frame by performing a critical phenomenology of her colonizing society, turning our attention to the particular, material, everyday situations in which the ideology of colonialism manifests, such as instances of grieving. I conclude by offering cautionary notes against potential responses to the colonial frame (inclusion, pity, and tolerance) while underscoring that the take-home value of Weil's practices and writings lies in their emphasis on self-critique, and in the critique of one's own nation-state in particular.[4]

THE COLONIAL FRAME

Like the frame of a painting, "frame" in Butler's sense editorializes the image it outlines, calling some features to more significance than others. And like the frame of the legal sense "to be framed," Butler's frame carries the connotation of guiding the viewer to interpretive conclusions, including judgments of guilt and decisions to punish. More than the setting of an art gallery or the scene of a courtroom, however, Butler is interested in the context of war. "War is framed," they write, "to control and heighten affect in relation to the differential grievability of lives."[5] They list the following as particular examples of frames of war: frames of photographs, framing a decision to go to war in the first place, the framing of immigration as the "war at home," and how sexual and feminist politics are framed in the language of war.[6] Through the term "grievability," they invite consideration of the conditions under which the loss of a life matters. This means more than the ordinary usage of "grief," which refers to a life that has been lived. A life only counts, Butler argues, if it *would be grieved*, were it lost. Grieving demonstrates that loss matters, and it does so in everyday events. At the birth of another, or in encountering another, there is an implicit understanding that, were the life of this other lost, it would be grieved. On this analysis, grievability is a *presupposition* for life that counts; it "precedes and makes possible the apprehension of the living being as living."[7] If a grievable life *would be* mourned, an ungrievable life, conversely, "cannot be mourned because it has never lived, that is, it has never counted as a life at all."[8]

Frames condition what is grievable, especially what is grievable in public and as a collectivity. For instance, frames give shape to a nation not only imagined but also "produced and sustained through powerful forms of media."[9] In the case of the U.S. invasion of Iraq, when U.S. soldiers died on the same day that other U.S. soldiers killed Iraqi civilians, the operation of the frame was present as U.S. news channels told only the story of the death of the soldiers, *our* soldiers. Targeted populations, then, are not quite lives. Here we see several features of frames through grievability: frames are active—"both jettisoning and presenting, and as doing both at once, in silence, without any visible sign of [their] operation."[10] They are selective, operating such that recognition of life occurs differentially, often according to race, sexuality, gender, nationality, or labor status. Further, suggesting that only certain lives matter—that only certain lives are worth mourning—frames are "politically saturated," themselves "operations of power."[11] Therefore, they are not neutral or merely descriptive but partisan and prescriptive; they "do not merely reflect on the material conditions of war, but are essential to the perpetually crafted *animus* of that material reality."[12] It is also crucial to understand that frames are *already* operative: certain lives are deemed worthy of grief, protection, attention, and so on, and other lives are not, because of *predominant* norms of recognizability that preexist any specific recognition.[13] Butler highlights this point: "[W]hether and how we respond to the suffering of others, how we formulate moral criticisms, how we articulate political analyses, depends upon a certain field of perceptible reality having already been established."[14]

In sum, frames seek "to contain, convey, and determine what is seen."[15] Crucially, they fail to accomplish the final action. Frames condition but do not determine appearance. The failure of the frame to function deterministically is due to its structure of iterability. That is, as the philosopher Jacques Derrida taught, frames must alter—must break with themselves—in order to reproduce themselves, and they do this over both space and time.[16] A photograph, for instance, circulates internationally: the reproduction of its frame means that it breaks from the context of when it was taken, traveling through media. To see a photo of an Israeli settlement on a computer at a café in Atlanta is at once a repetition of the frame of the photograph (it is the same photograph) and a differentiation (it is seen in a different place, at a different time, by a different person).

The frame also fails to determine what appears because something always exceeds it—"something occurs that does not conform to our established understanding of things."[17] In light of the importance, or gravity, of the already operative norms of the frame, some "subjects" are not recognized as subjects, some "lives" are not quite considered lives, some "humans" are not thought of as humans. "In what sense does life, then," Butler asks, "always exceed the normative conditions of its recognizability?"[18] The point of the question is understood in providing concrete answers: in Weil's France, the colonized subject is a life that exceeds the recognition of French citizens. This is also true—and this is Butler's point—with respect to those in countries the United States has recently invaded vis-à-vis members of the imagined and produced U.S. collectivity. In other words, the colonized subject is not really a life at all, according to the French or U.S. colonial frame.[19]

Overall, in *Frames of War* Butler is advancing "an historically contingent ontology" that works to denaturalize (colonial) practices of grieving and, more generally, of affect.[20] It is not the case that the recognition of and attention to certain people is a natural occurrence. Rather, this recognition and attention is the result of a long process of state-promoted normative schemes. "[C]asting emotion as a basis for naturalized social or moral consensus," literary theorist Rei Terada points out, is an "ideological convenience."[21] To understand the colonial frame's contingency is to understand how it is an ideological convenience (not a natural occurrence). In addition to guiding this understanding of the regulation of affect, what is at stake for Butler is a response that could contribute to "a new trajectory of affect" that might speak to "knowing how we might respond effectively to suffering at a distance."[22] While affective responses "call upon and enact certain interpretive frames," they can also "call into question the taken-for-granted character of those frames, and in that way provide the affective conditions for social critique."[23]

We can read Butler's critique of ideology as a way to understand Weil's critique of French colonization. What is rarely seen or told, Butler remarks, is that certain forms of state power are embedded in the frame, such as maps and directives—of military operations and, indeed, of what we attend to in everyday life.[24] In her writings on colonialism, Weil revealed these power-laden forms by suggesting the contingency of the colonial frame. In turn, she called into question what decolonial philosopher Nelson Maldonado-Torres has called the naturalization of war in the West, meaning "the radical suspension or displacement of ethical and political relationships in favor of the propagation of a peculiar death ethic that renders massacre and different forms of genocide as natural."[25] In addressing the ideology of colonialism, I will suggest that Weil's response to the affliction of those colonized by her country, particularly the way in which her shame at this colonization motivated her political engagements, exemplifies the move from affective response to social critique.

SIMONE WEIL'S CRITICAL PHENOMENOLOGY

In 1930 Weil read Louis Roubaud's exposé of the Yen Bay massacre in French Indochina, published in *Le Petit Parisien*. In the article she learned of the conditions of the colonized—"their destitution, their slavery, the insolence of the whites that went unsanctioned" (SWC 47/EHP II, 102). "I will never forget the moment," she writes, "when I felt and understood the tragedy of colonization" (SWC 47/EHP II, 102, translation modified). "Since that day," she goes on, "I have been ashamed of my country [*Depuis ce jour, j'ai honte de mon pays*]" (SWC 47/EHP II, 102, translation modified). Yet being ashamed was never enough for Weil.[26] Shame, instead, served as motivation to do more; becoming conscious of colonialism caused her to call into question her own practices as well as those of other citizens, including fellow comrades on the Left, in her country. This is an inversion of the traditional function of shame, which is indexed to power in the State. Usually, the philosopher Martha Nussbaum explains, "the dominant group characterizes itself as 'normal' and the divergent group as shameful, asking them to blush for who they are."[27] Weil, instead, interrogated the norms of her own dominant group.

Weil problematized her own situation and nation-state by performing a critical phenomenology of colonial society. By "phenomenology," I mean a method of analysis that suspends an uncritical acceptance of the natural(ized) attitude of the colonial frame, sees concepts as interpretive and embodied practices, and proceeds through increasingly sophisticated descriptions of lived experience.[28] Phenomenology begins from the claim that meanings *appear* to us. Because the natural attitude, here the colonial frame, takes meanings for granted, as inherent in experience, it does not investigate structures of appearance. A phenomenological approach, by contrast, takes meanings as *accomplishments* and, in turn, investigates the values and conditions that allow for any given meaning to be achieved. It follows that if those conditioning structures can be changed, so too would the meanings—which are always already interpretations—be altered. That is, if the political and social life of a collectivity changes, it will frame events differently.

A first, critical phenomenological step toward this alternative framing is to call into question how experience appears to us. The modifier "critical" suggests, in addition to the interrogation of appearances, work being done to cultivate alternative social forms. Here I follow the philosopher Lisa Guenther in her description of critical phenomenology as twofold, that is, as "both a philosophical practice of reflecting on the transcendental and material structures that make experience possible and meaningful" and "a political practice of 'restructuring the world' in order to generate new and liberatory possibilities for meaningful experience and existence."[29] Weil's writings are *phenomenological* in calling into question which experiences appear as grievable and tragic through the colonial frame and *critical* in essaying, beyond a posture of *aporia*, alternative political arrangements in France. I will read Weil's critical phenomenology through three of her writings on colonialism: "Morocco, or a Lesson in Theft," "Blood is Flowing in Tunisia," and "New Facts about the Colonial Problem in the French Empire."

In "Morocco, or A Lesson in Theft," from early 1937, Weil parodies the French reaction to a threat to its territory, the "sacred soil" and "fatherland" (SWC 31/EHP II, 93). Many French citizens argue that "a territory that has belonged to France since 1911 is French by right for all eternity"; indeed, she continues, "that's what appears even more clearly if one looks at the history of Morocco" (SWC 32/EHP II, 94). Like imperial powers and police forces in our time, France diagnosed a situation as starting to be problematic only when white lives were threatened, sending troops to Morocco in light of "the beginnings of unrest, which was putting the lives of Europeans in danger" (SWC 33/EHP II, 95). She writes critically of the discourse of "security": France "promised to withdraw [the troops] as soon as security was reestablished" (SWC 33/EHP II, 95). And she observes that France cares more for prestige than for international law (a claim equally true of the U.S. invasion of Iraq).[30] She follows her jabs at French society in "Morocco" with a bigger cut at French social life in her 1937 "Blood is Flowing in Tunisia."

Weil begins that essay by emphasizing blood itself. It is blood that is at stake in colonialism, with the blood of some receiving more attention than that of others.[31] Whereas French workers were regarded by the President, she observes that "the millions of workers who suffer, exhaust themselves, and despair throughout the French Empire had been forgotten" (SWC 41/EHP II, 97). "We'd all forgotten them [*Mais les millions de prolétaires des colonies, nous tous, nous les avions oubliés*]," she adds (SWC 41/EHP II, 97). The reason for this forgetting is distance. Here Weil recounts the customary view: "Everyone knows that the magnitude of problems and people, the seriousness of injustices, the intensity of suffering, all diminish in proportion to their distance" (SWC 42/EHP II, 97). The tradition of Western moral philosophy claims that distance diminishes empathy and attention: the stoic *oikeiosis*, for instance, suggests that concern radiates outward, becoming weaker as it disperses farther and farther away. Weil is ultimately arguing against any easy employment of this naturalized tradition, even if she acknowledges with clear eyes that "[d]istance diminishes the weight on our minds of acts of injustice and oppression, in the same manner as it acts on gravity with respect to objects" (SWC 42/EHP II, 98). She describes how racialized conceptions of others make the French think that others are inured to suffering and, moreover, are completely Other, "not made like us" (SWC 42/EHP II, 98). Their pain "is not really very gripping," unless it is sensational—"massacres . . . that speak to the imagination" (SWC 42/EHP II, 98). She then asks a question of "our country," that is, of herself and her fellow citizens: "But tears shed in silence, mute despair, revolt suppressed under the pressure of constraint, hopeless resignation, exhaustion, slow death—does all that count?" (SWC 42/EHP II, 98). Even though our country has responsibility for this affliction—even though "millions of human beings . . . from the depths of an abyss of slavery and affliction turned their eyes toward us"—it does not bear on us, does not cause hesitation (SWC 43/EHP II, 98). "Such deaths don't count; they aren't real deaths" (SWC 42/EHP II, 98).

* * *

To reiterate: the problem is not simply distance, meaning that certain, far-away affliction "exceeds the capacity of . . . imagination" and by extension exceeds faculties of attention and empathy, but the problem is also that workers in other countries are racialized such that they are considered "as beings of another species" (SWC 43/EHP II, 98). Colonial power manifests as a manipulation of vision and feeling: the selectivity of the frame is preconditioned such that colonized subjects are invisible, and when they appear, such as through forcing some living in French Indochina to "volunteer" to labor in France, they appear as of another species, accused of Otherness beyond concern (including dialogue, love, disagreement, play, and other forms of shared life). This is, as the post-colonial theorist Gayatri Spivak puts it, an "epistemic violence"—"the remotely orchestrated, far-flung, and heterogenous project to constitute the colonial subject as Other"—that affects people materially.[32]

For both Spivak and Weil, the subaltern, in affliction, is mute. They differ in terms of both specificity and response, however. Spivak's emphasis on the *gendered* subaltern is more particular than Weil's universality allows. And whereas Spivak remains critical of French intellectuals' attempts to represent subalterns, Weil would write in the 1942–1943 essay "Human Personality": "In order to provide an armour for the afflicted [*les malheureux*], one must put into their mouths only those words whose rightful abode is in heaven, beyond heaven, in the other world" (SWA 86/EL 27). This call to put words into the mouths of the afflicted raises significant concerns for the post- and decolonial thinker. It certainly reflects one of Weil's limitations. She is at her most helpful not when she is suggesting how to help the afflicted but when she keeps her self-critique focused on the practices of French citizens.

Weil observes that, due to such racialized conditioning of affect, the empathy of the bourgeoisie does not pass far beyond the beggar in the street, namely, the French person who looks like they do. And while Butler reminds us that implicit frames of recognizability are in play anytime I recognize someone as "like me," Weil considers the French response to precarity—to what Butler describes as "that politically induced condition" in which the colonized are "differentially exposed to injury, violence, and death"—in more simple terms: it is stupidity.[33] "Does the bourgeoisie at all levels manifest its stupidity, its brutality, its narrow-mindedness," Weil asks her readers, "primarily by getting interested in a particular crime, a suicide, a railway accident, and ignoring the fact that millions of lives are slowly crushed, ground down, and destroyed by the everyday workings of the social machine?" (SWC 43/EHP II, 98). She employs this question as a rhetorical device to set up her readers. After all, she writes, "*we*"—and she means those on the Left—"have the same mentality as the bourgeoisie" (SWC 42/EHP II, 98). She continues poignantly: "Every one of us can see one of the culprits by looking in the mirror" (SWC 43/EHP II, 99).[34]

* * *

Weil's critical phenomenology took on additional historical and political nuance in her late 1938 "New Facts about the Colonial Problem in the French

Empire." She links colonialism to her concept of force from the opening sentences:

> The problems regarding colonization can be stated above all in terms of force. Colonization nearly always begins by the exercise of force in its purest form, that is, by conquest. A people, overcome through force of arms, suddenly has to submit to the control of foreigners of another color, another language, a completely different culture, convinced of their own superiority. (SWC 66/EHP II, 111)

Colonization is forced imposition, both concrete, for instance in territorial conquest, and conceptual, for instance in the introduction of hierarchies (inferior/superior). After presenting the colonial problem as a problem of force, Weil turns to the question of how to improve the situation. "One of the ways that can be imagined," she suggests, "is the birth of a movement of opinion in the colonizing nation against the appalling injustices imposed on the colonies" (SWC 67/EHP II, 112). Indeed, in a State that promotes ostensibly universal rights, "that proclaims an ideal of freedom and humanity," "[i]t would seem easy to provoke such a movement of opinion" (SWC 67/EHP II, 112). But this is not the case, she continues soberly: "Generosity hardly ever extends in any people as far as making an effort to discover the injustices committed in their name" (SWC 68/EHP II, 112). Revolt is a second possibility, but it is unlikely to succeed, she claims, and even if it did, it is likely that "constraint, exhaustion, and hunger" would remain "as great as under foreign domination" (SWC 68/EHP II, 113). Thus independence—"doubtless a good thing"—would be rendered "meaningless" (SWC 68/EHP II, 113). Weil ultimately endorses a third way starting from the fact that "the colonizing nation [has] an interest in the progressive emancipation of her colonies, and that she be conscious of this interest" (SWC 68/EHP II, 113).

This third way, Weil admits, is an improbable solution, thwarted by "the ignorance in France concerning the facts of the situation" (SWC 71/EHP II, 115), what Spivak calls "the sanctioned ignorance that every critic of imperialism must chart."[35] Indeed, comfortable citizens of a State do not take as seriously what offends justice as what threatens their personal security. Weil acknowledges that her endorsed plan would be rejected by radicals. To the revolutionaries, this third way, this "solution," "bears the indelible defect of reformism" (SWC 70/EHP II, 115). To the decolonial thinker, this third way also bears the troubling defect of paternalism and gradualism, which militate against independence and liberation. Indeed, the philosopher who wants to think alongside Weil with a view toward decolonial efforts must reject the continual hesitation that one can hear in her advocacy toward "partial emancipation"; for the Weil of "New Facts," in her own words, "There is no question of suddenly making the colonies independent states" (SWC 70, 69/EHP II, 114).

It is hard to read such a theoretical commentary wary of independence as anything but a denial of the self-determination of colonized peoples. My view is that, as readers of Weil, recognizing the limitations of some of her problematic formulations does not mean we have to discard her insights. Her arguments against immediate independence do not nullify her critical contribution, but we gloss over those arguments at our own peril. Indeed, if we overlook them, we risk repeating their mistakes. One reason her analysis is limited is that, in considering French colonization through her own perspective on potential paths from the position of a distanced and learned theorist, she does not sufficiently, as Maldonado-Torres puts it, "highlight the epistemic relevance of the enslaved and colonized search for humanity" and thus does not—at least in this moment in the 1930s—heed a call "to open up the sources for thinking and to break up the apartheid of theoretical domains," a call Weil would no doubt affirm.[36]

In the final instance, I think Weil is instructive not in her prescribed reform but in her refusal to accept an aporetic posture that would dwell, and remain, in the difficulty of essaying another way. "Regarding the colonies," she writes in a 1938–1939 fragment, "it is not sufficient to make do with a question mark" (SWC 74/EHP II, 117). What to bear in mind, then, when offering a self-critical response to the question of colonialism? Writing in 1939, in an unfinished essay titled "Reflections on Barbarism," she states: "I believe that the concept of force must be made central in any attempt to think clearly about human relations [*Je ne crois pas que l'on puisse former des pensées claires sur les rapports humains tant qu'on n'aura pas mis au centre la notion de force*]" (SE 143/EHP I, 51).[37] It is also in this essay that she writes, "[W]e are always barbarous toward the weak unless we make an effort of generosity that is as rare as genius" (SE 143/EHP I, 51). Here she inverts tradition once again: it is the forceful who are barbarous, and she implicates herself in the barbarism of the powerful, a move especially noteworthy given her preferred position on the threshold or margins of any collectivity. *We* are barbarous, she insists. This sense of the forceful as barbarous, as well as this implication of self, substantiate my claim that Weil teaches us—we who are citizens of colonizing powers—something about calling into question colonial ideology.[38]

Weil presents a real way to respond to the colonial frame (and the force that follows it) to the extent that she focuses not on the improvement of a situation "over there," itself a move according to a colonial trajectory, but precisely as she moves through self-critique: she feels shame toward her country, and she shed shameful tears over the hunger of others, over those, according to the colonial frame, who are "something living that is other than life."[39] But tears are not autotelic. What is more important politically is her critical phenomenology, her resolute interrogation into ideologically conditioned affective attachments. Weil shows that the colonial frame can be unveiled when it is denaturalized—when one sees both how what it frames is not natural but historically contingent (e.g., the possession of Morocco) and how it shapes our material and affective practices (e.g., what we consider dispossession as related to whose tears we attend to and whose we forget). In exposing through phenomenology the achievement or accomplishment (and not the "natural" presence) of the colonial frame and what appears through it, Weil saw through "the ideological construction of a world that is so false that the real appears to be unbelievable."[40] She stayed with the trouble of attending to reality instead of a-voiding it, in A. Rebecca Rozelle-Stone's neologism, where "a-voidances" are "flights from reality and from suffering."[41] Still, as Butler notes, "[a]n ethical attitude does not spontaneously arrive as soon as the usual interpretive frameworks are destroyed, and no pure moral conscience emerges once the shackles of everyday interpretation have been thrown off."[42] "On the contrary," she continues in a call to political engagement, "it is only by challenging the dominant media that certain kinds of lives may become visible or knowable in their precariousness."[43]

POLITICS AND CONTESTATION

Thinking with Butler and Weil, I want to issue three cautions regarding what might be taken up as challenges to dominant media. It would be a mistake to pose the next question as how to expand recognition so that it encompasses what was previously abjected. This approach does not change the normative conditions at play in the colonial frame, but only extends them; it treats the problem as one of inclusion instead of transformation.[44] It would also be a mistake to think that this situation calls for pity. Summed up in the cliché "giving voice to the voiceless," pity is a "soft arrogance" that manifests in "contrived gasps and tears."[45] It features three key defects: its position of imperial power; its colonial epistemological drive to comprehend and to consume others; and, thirdly, as philosophers Lucian Stone and Jason Mohaghegh explain, "pity is not an actual affect but simply the unspontaneous ideological façade of an affect."[46] Pity is to be expected in the colonial frame. It is at once an exacerbation of the problem and its most salient illustration, obviating self-critique in its petty display. In addition to rejecting expansion and pity, Butler and Weil are calling for an orientation beyond tolerance. As Butler comments, tolerance assumes subjects "differentiated from the start," such that "both positions get defined in terms of their putatively conflictual relation with one another, at which point we come to know very little about either category or the sites of their sociological convergence."[47]

Instead of inspiring a just balance, tolerance functions according to the logic of which bodies matter in the colonial frame; it "orders identity according to its requirements" and thereby uproots, "effac[ing] . . . complex cultural realities."[48] Ultimately, tolerance "regulates aversion," in Wendy Brown's words, presupposing contempt for another while asserting the ethical "virtues" of the tolerant.[49] In sum, inclusion, pity, and tolerance are not attentive responses, nor do they call into question how my everyday actions perpetuate the affliction of others (whom I in turn pity, tolerate, "give" to in philanthropy, and otherwise approach through unchallenged colonial power relations). If there is a difference between pity and compassion, for Weil that difference would lie not only in the need to place oneself alongside another in compassion (i.e., to break from one's social class) but also to remain self-implicated and self-critical in that placement and break.

How, then, to respond attentively to those, near and at a distance, whose lives are not considered grievable? How to understand, interrogate, and exacerbate the contestations and fractures of the colonial frame? Here we must recall, learning from Weil and Butler together, that in a colonizing society the colonial frame is already operative, that the force concomitant with it is predominant and self-perpetuating, and that the frame has already worked to constitute a certain subject and its Other. "The point is not to eradicate the conditions of one's own production," however, Butler writes, "but to assume responsibility for living a life that contests the determining power of that production; in other words, that makes good use of the iterability of the productive norms and, hence, of their fragility and transformability."[50] As Weil understood from the war-fatigued Greeks in the *Iliad*, as the political theorist Roberto Esposito points out, "it is precisely because they know that force covers the entire canvas that they can direct their gaze to the frame as well as to the internal fractures of the canvas."[51]

In short, from Butler and Weil we can learn how to struggle: to implicate ourselves in our country's violences and to own up to the predominance of colonial force as it informs who we take ourselves to be. The alternative is to avoid reality, to hold fast to the colonially framed and ideologically informed claim that there are prestigious spheres outside of politics.[52] If we betray our political commitments most saliently through our emotions, most poignantly through what we grieve, then one reiteration could move to cultivate an alternative affect in ways that deepen the fragile fractures of the frame.[53] To consider grieving differently, in a way unrecognized according to the dominant, colonial frame, could open onto practices of liberty, attention, and responsibility in the spirit of Weil.

To be clear, grieving differently does not itself somehow bring about political changes in line with decolonial aims. To make such a claim would be a betrayal to Weil's materialist analysis. What I want to suggest, rather, is that if citizens of the United States and other colonial countries today, like the French in Weil's time, were to grieve differently, such vibrant emotional practices would be the result of, and contribute to, other fundamental shifts in our polities, such as a move from nationalist to internationalist frames of conflicts. Our emotional lives follow from our political lives and vice versa. While emotions such as resentment, anger, and ethnocentric feeling remain central to fascisms and nationalisms today, attending to our emotional patterns could also raise awareness about our political loyalties, and from a position of raised consciousness, we can begin to reorient how we frame our ethical and political obligations. We would then acknowledge that many of our practices of grieving follow the age-old pattern of stoic *oikeiosis*. We would see that, just like how we root for our city's professional baseball team and then, in a larger circle, our country at the Olympics, we grieve primarily for our families and then for our church members and then for our fellow citizens, and so on. Denaturalizing this frame of obligations and binds, and starting conversations with those families, church groups, and so on about our now-recognized loyalties, we can reframe our webs of emotion into wider solidarities. Whether these newfound solidarities should proceed on lines of shared humanity, human rights, internationalist political parties, or universal compassion is the subject of the following chapters. To deepen our understanding of political subjectivity on Weil's account, in the next chapter, I explain how she theorized the relationship between politics and the self.

NOTES

1. Inese Radzins has noted that "Weil pointed to . . . the dual nature of France's destruction—not only in oppressing others, but also by sanctioning this destruction through various policies at home" (Inese Radzins, "Simone Weil's Social Philosophy: Toward a Post-Colonial Ethic" in *New Topics in Feminist Philosophy of Religion: Contestations and Transcendence Incarnate*, ed. Pamela Sue Anderson [Dordrecht: Springer, 2010], 71). A future site of Weil studies lies in placing Weil in dialogue with decolonial contemporaries and continuations, including W. E. B. Du Bois's treatment of the endurances of colonialism in his 1945 *Color and Democracy: Colonies and Peace* and the Caribbean diagnosis that the two fundamental aspects of France's relation to the world are universal freedom and colonialism—see Patrick Chamoiseau and Édouard Glissant's "When the Walls Fall: Is National Identity an Outlaw?"

2. This chapter is derived in part from the book *Simone Weil, Beyond Ideology?* Published December 17, 2020, copyright Springer Nature, available online https://doi .org/10.1007/978-3-030-48401-9_7. See Benjamin P. Davis, "The Colonial Frame: Judith Butler and Simone Weil on Force and Grief," in *Simone Weil, Beyond Ideology*, eds. Sophie Bourgault and Julie Daigle (London: Palgrave MacMillan: 2020), 125–42, reproduced with permission of Palgrave Macmillan.

3. My emphasis on Weil's analysis of emotion challenges her reputation as generally lacking in sensitivity and feeling. Deborah Nelson observes that women philosophers such as Weil "have been perceived as psychologically cold rather than engaged in an ethical project with different assumptions" (Nelson, *Tough Enough*, 9). Making a point related to Nelson's, Sophie Bourgault observes that myriad of Weil's biographies feature "the disturbing subtext . . . that it is *particularly* strange for a woman to eschew romantic love, children, or sex" (Bourgault, "Beyond," 1).

4. Akeel Bilgrami details the virtues of an intellectual's criticizing their own nation-state in the following terms: "I find it not only understandable, but honorable, if someone speaking and writing in America finds it important to *stress much more* the wrongs of the American government and its allies and clients, like Israel, Saudi Arabia, Egypt, Pakistan (now even India), Indonesia under Suharto, Chile under Pinochet, and so on, rather than speak obsessively, as it is so often done, about the wrongs done by Muslim terrorists or Islamic theocratic regimes or, for that matter, Cuba and North Korea. But if the same person was speaking or writing, say, in the Palestinian territories or in Arab or Middle Eastern newspapers, it would be far more admirable if he were to criticize Hamas or Islamic regimes like Iran's. So also, unlike the many who were abusive toward him for not doing so, I find it entirely honorable that Sartre, living in Paris in the Cold War ethos, refused to spend his time criticizing the Soviet Union and instead criticized Western governments for the most part" (Akeel Bilgrami, *Secularism, Identity, and Enchantment* [Cambridge, MA: Harvard University Press, 2014], 96).

5. Judith Butler, *Frames of War: When Is Life Grievable?* (New York: Verso, 2009), 26.

6. Ibid.

7. Ibid., 15.

8. Ibid., 38.

9. Ibid., 125, 47.

10. Ibid., 73.

11. Ibid., 1.

12. Ibid., 26.

13. Ibid., 50.

14. Ibid., 63–64.

15. Ibid., 10.

16. Jacques Derrida, *Margins of Philosophy* (Chicago: University of Chicago Press, 1982), 315.

17. Butler, *Frames*, 9.

18. Ibid., 4.

19. Butler's consideration of precarious and grievable lives is different from "bare life" in the political philosophy of Giorgio Agamben: "the lives in question are not cast outside the polis in a state of radical exposure, but bound and constrained by power relations in a situation of forcible exposure" (Butler, *Frames*, 29). Thus we can begin to place Weil and Butler in dialogue. Weil, too, would focus on State-sponsored force. For an important book on this subject, see Joy James, *Resisting State Violence: Radicalism, Gender, and Race in U.S. Culture.*

20. Butler, *Frames*, 4.

21. Rei Terada, *Feeling in Theory: Emotion after the "Death of the Subject"* (Cambridge, MA: Harvard University Press, 2001), 4.

22. Butler, *Frames*, 11, 63.

23. Ibid., 34–35.

24. Ibid., 72–74. For a consideration of those mappings, see e.g., the excellent collection of poetry *Victims of a Map*. In one of those poems, "Travel Tickets," Samih al-Qasim writes: "On the day you kill me / You'll find in my pocket / Travel tickets / To peace, / To the fields and the rain, / To people's conscience. / Don't waste the tickets" (Samih al-Qasim, "Travel Tickets," in *Victims of a Map: A Bilingual Anthology of Arabic Poetry*, ed. Abdullah al-Udhari [London: Saqi Books, 1984], 59).

25. Nelson Maldonado-Torres, *Against War: Views from the Underside of Modernity* (Durham, NC: Duke University Press, 2008), xi.

26. In both this essay, "Who is Guilty of Anti-French Plots?," and her "Letter to the Indochinese," Weil writes about how, when she first read about the actions of the French in what was then called Indochina, she stopped eating—she could not eat and "stomach" the news at the same time. In fact, reading about the actions of "her" country caused her physical pain, she notes. A reading of Weil that is rarely considered is that her practices around food could be exemplary for a philosopher and in particular for a teacher of ethics. Perhaps to the extent that we are able to read news about child labor in the mines that is needed for our electronic devices, about vaccine apartheid, about forcing Indigenous children onto residential schools, and about so much else in our world marked by a global division of labor, perhaps to that extent we have accustomed ourselves to, or gotten comfortable with, living in a colonial world. Weil's (extreme?) response might just be a pedagogical one: she teaches us how to become unaccustomed to daily life in the (colonial) present.

27. Martha Nussbaum, *Political Emotions: Why Love Matters for Justice* (Cambridge, MA: Belknap Press: An Imprint of Harvard University Press, 2013), 360.

28. For this approach to phenomenology, see Eduardo Mendieta, *Global Fragments: Globalizations, Latinamericanisms, and Critical Theory* (Albany: State University of New York Press, 2007), 37. I call Weil's analysis phenomenology, further, because of how it, in Anthony Steinbock's words, "takes us beyond a subject-object dichotomy often attributed to Western philosophical thought insofar as givenness is not necessarily attached to the appearing of an object over against a subject" (Anthony Steinbock, *Phenomenology and Mysticism: The Verticality of Religious Experience* [Indianapolis: Indiana University Press, 2007], 2). Indeed, Steinbock continues, "[w]e are involved in the very course of our experiences. We hardly notice them when they flow on concordantly without disruption or when everything works harmoniously" (ibid., 2–3). For more on emerging discussion of "critical phenomenology," see Lisa Guenther, *Solitary Confinement: Social Death and Its Afterlives* (Minneapolis: University of Minnesota Press, 2013).

29. Lisa Guenther, "A Critical Phenomenology of Solidarity and Resistance in 2013 California Prison Hunger Strikes," in *Body/Self/Other: The Phenomenology of Social Encounters*, eds. Luna Dolezal and Danielle Petherbridge (Albany: State University of New York Press, 2017), 49.

30. "Prestige" is a technical term in Weil. She had worked out its connection to violence and fascism in her 1936 "Do We Have to Grease Our Combat Boots," writing: "One must choose between prestige and peace. And whether one claims to believe in the fatherland, democracy, or revolution, the policy of prestige means war" (FW 258/EHP II, 29). I will return to this point in my final chapter.

31. Substituting "political" for "theological" and "colonialism" for "Christianity" in Gil Anidjar's political-theological text *Blood*, we read: "[T]here is nothing natural about blood, and the confusion as to its literal or figurative status (a key site of difference 'between bloods'), its physiological or [political] existence, is crucial to understand [colonialism], to consider and reflect upon it" (Gil Anidjar, *Blood: A Critique of Christianity* [New York: Columbia University Press, 2014], 257). Blood could open new forms of relation, kin, attention across borders: "It *can* so break and might therefore *engender* new contexts; it has, in the form of new notions of kinship and of race or of novel, massive, and massively hailed and barely interrogated practices (circulation, donation, and transfusion, for instance)" (ibid., ix).

32. Gayatri Chakravorty Spivak, "Can the Subaltern Speak?," in *Colonial Discourse and Post-Colonial Theory*, eds. Patrick Williams and Laura Chrisman (New York: Columbia University Press, 1994), 75, 76.

33. Butler, *Frames*, 36, 26.

34. The U.S. Left today remains culpable in, for instance, the reprehensible claim to closed borders in the name of U.S. workers. See Angela Nagle, "The Left Case against Open Borders," *American Affairs* 2, no. 4 (2018).

35. Spivak, "Can the Subaltern Speak?," 86.

36. Maldonado-Torres, *Against War*, 7.

37. Pétrement, *Simone Weil*, 361.

38. Butler writes tongue-in-cheek, not unlike Weil at times, that the photos of U.S. torture at Abu Ghraib show that "in an effort to win the clash of civilizations and subject the ostensible barbarians to our civilizing mission," the U.S. "has rid itself so beautifully of our own barbarism" (Butler, *Frames*, 84–85).

39. Butler, *Frames*, 15.

40. Roberto Esposito, *The Origin of the Political: Hannah Arendt or Simone Weil?*, trans. Vincenzo Binetti and Gareth Williams (New York: Fordham University Press, 2017), 3.

41. Rozelle-Stone, *"Le Déracinement* of Attention," 101, 104. For a discussion of the nation-state's collective avoidance, see Mahmoud Darwish, *Journal of an Ordinary Grief*, trans. Ibrahim Muhawi (New York: Archipelago Books, 2010).

42. Butler, *Frames*, 51.

43. Ibid.

44. This caution is in line with the decolonial philosopher Enrique Dussel's call for political transformation: "The excluded should not be merely *included* in the *old* system—as this would be to introduce the Other into the Same—but rather ought to participate as equals in a *new institutional moment* (the *new* political order)" (Enrique Dussel, *Twenty Theses on Politics* [Durham, NC: Duke University Press, 2008], 89).

45. Lucian Stone and Jason Mohaghegh, "Introduction: Outsider Imperatives," in *Manifestos for World Thought*, eds. Lucian Stone and Jason Bahbak Mohaghegh (Lanham, MD: Rowman & Littlefield International, 2017), x.

46. Ibid.

47. Butler, *Frames*, 140, 143.

48. Ibid., 143.

49. For the function of tolerance in a colonial context, cf. Wendy Brown, *Regulating Aversion: Tolerance in the Age of Identity and Empire* (Princeton, NJ: Princeton University Press, 2018).

50. Ibid., 170–171. This resonates with what Alessia Ricciardi has called Weil's "negative politics," meaning "a kind of negative thinking with respect to institutional, ideologically formalized politics, a skepticism that nevertheless eschews nihilism" (Alessia Ricciardi, "From Decreation to Bare Life: Weil, Agamben, and the Impolitical," *Diacritics* 39, no. 2 [2009]: 76–77).

51. Esposito, *Origin*, 49.

52. In "About the Problems in the French Empire," written in exile from New York in mid- to late 1942, Weil was still thinking about French colonialism, observing: "There lives in the soul of all men a burning hunger for freedom which, as a source of energy, is more precious than coal or oil" (SWC 90). Weil thus demands an inversion of priorities by connecting turning on the lights, driving to work, or flying to a prestigious international academic conference—all of which rely on coal or oil—to the liberty of some and the oppression of others. "Politics is everywhere," Edward Said adds; "there can be no escape into the realms of pure art and thought or, for that matter, into the realm of disinterested objectivity or transcendental theory. Intellectuals are *of* their time, herded along by the mass politics of representations embodied by the information or media industry, capable of resisting those only by disputing the images, [frames,] official narratives, justifications of power circulated by an increasingly powerful media—and not only media but whole trends of thought that maintain the status quo, keep things within an acceptable and sanctioned perspective on actuality" (Edward Said, *Representations of the Intellectual: The 1993 Reith Lectures* [New York: Vintage, 1994], 21–22).

53. My emphasis on intention and effort here, to be clear, resonates less with Derrida's reiteration and more with Sartre's owned sense of responsibility in *Sketch for a Theory of the Emotions*.

Chapter 3

Critique of the (Neoliberal) Self

What are the implications, for politics and ethics, of the ongoing neoliberal moment we are living through? Philosopher Jessica Whyte has argued that "[w]e cannot understand the neoliberal victory if we view it only in economic terms."[1] "The success of neoliberalism," she goes on, "was not predicated merely on its arguments for the superior efficiency of market, or its challenges to the economics of socialist planning."[2] More than that, Whyte concludes, "neoliberals pioneered a series of political arguments about the dangers of wealth redistribution, interference with the market and mass participation in politics, especially in the postcolony, that helped legitimise austerity and the crushing of Third Worldist demands for global wealth redistribution."[3] In this chapter, by considering the neoliberal victory in ethical terms, I build on Whyte's bold attempt to understand the extensive ramifications of neoliberalism. I argue that Weil's writings on literature offer a corrective to neoliberalism's ethics of resilience and self-improvement. Weil's conceptualization of the self is an alternative to the facile neoliberal understanding of the human condition. Neoliberal ethics posit a self that eschews dark nights of the soul for the sake of entrepreneurial self-improvement, a self that remains obsessed with its ability to overcome social, political, and economic barriers. Weil's portrait of the human condition, by contrast, presents a sense of the self that tarries with the existential difficulties of finitude, pain, and solitude. To make this argument, I read two of Weil's essays from the early 1940s. Sometime between October 1941 and February 1942, she wrote "Literature and Morals," which was not published by *Cahiers du Sud* until 1944.[4] It was also in 1941 that she wrote a letter to *Cahiers du Sud* called "Responsibilities of Literature"—a letter which would not be published until 1951. These essays are the focus of this chapter.

In response to this focus, my reader might wonder to what extent Weil's discussion of literature belongs in a book on Weil's political philosophy that starts from Weil's relationship to collectivity. There are two answers to that question. The first is that, in the 1940s, Weil developed a history of her present that understood writers as a kind of polity-directing collectivity. She would extend her commentary on the relationship between writers and collectivity into *The Need for Roots*, claiming with some degree of criticism that "[n]ever so much as in our age have they [writers] claimed the role of directors of conscience and exercised it" (NR 24/24). The second answer is that one of Weil's contributions to political philosophy is how she links one's sense of self to one's political commitments. Resonant with the Platonic dialogues that she kept close in her thinking, her theological writings criticize a sense of self that tries to will itself toward all-too-human ends, such as gaining power, without a proper orientation to what is absent from our unjust world. Her political writings—from her early conceptualization of the means-ends reversal that occurs in struggles for power, formulated in her 1934 "Reflections Concerning the Causes of Liberty and Social Oppression," to her connections early in *The Need for Roots* between the orientation of individuals' souls to the flourishing of a polity—issue the same critique.

Importantly, Weil maintained a robust intellectual life even under persecution and living in a state of exile. While the focus of this book is on her political writings, in this chapter I also treat Weil's activities in Marseilles to demonstrate the interplay of compassion and contemplation that guided her political life. In Marseilles she continued her wide inquiries into aesthetics and metaphysics even as State persecution narrowed her life. I read Weil's publishing in *Cahiers du Sud*, a Marseilles-based literary magazine important to the intellectual lives of French thinkers working under conditions of occupation, as part of her understanding of the need for varieties of thinking under repression.[5]

INTERNAL EXILE

On June 13, 1940, Weil and her parents went to the Gare de Lyon to board a train that was already full of passengers. They were fleeing persecution based on their being Jewish. Weil's brother, André, speculated that they were allowed to board only because Mme. Weil said M. Weil was the convoy's doctor.[6] Whatever the reason, they took the train to Nevers, where in a miller's house Weil started to become accustomed to sleeping on the floor, a habit she maintained until she was hospitalized in London. The Weil family then started to walk back to Paris, having read a leaflet demanding people return to their homes. They changed plans only upon meeting a former pupil of Simone's on the street, and in turn they headed to Vichy by way of a garage owner who offered to take them in his car to the unoccupied zone.[7] Writing from Vichy on August 19, Weil petitioned the Ministry of Education for a teaching position either abroad or in the colonies.[8] Waiting for a reply, she asked a contact to get from her briefcase in Paris "a prose piece, very long, typewritten, whose title I forget, but it has a quotation from Spinoza as an epigraph. It is essentially an analysis of political and social oppression, its permanent causes, its mechanism, and its present forms. It dates from 1934."[9] She was, of course, referencing "Reflections Concerning the Causes of Liberty and Social Oppression."[10] At this time, Weil thought she would go to Algiers, or to Morocco, or even to England via Portugal.[11] Instead, before September 15, 1940, Weil and her parents went from Toulouse to Marseilles, the main gathering point for those attempting to flee France.[12] In October 1940 she moved with her parents to 8 rue de Catalans in Marseilles. To this apartment Adèle Dubreuil, the family housekeeper, sent three (the quantity allowed) cases across the demarcation line. In these cases she included Weil's manuscripts and books.[13]

Weil had been appointed to teach at Constantine, a French *département* in Algeria, starting October 1, 1940, but this information never reached her.[14] In early October or November, she wrote a letter to the Minister of Public Education. In this letter she attributes her not receiving a post to the Vichy "Statutory Regulation on Jews," which prevented Jews from working as teachers. She further claims she has not inherited the Jewish religion and that she does not and never has participated in any religion. She cites her education and notes "if there is a religious tradition that I regard as my patrimony, it is the Catholic tradition," adding "The Christian, French, Hellenic tradition is mine; the Hebrew tradition is foreign to me; no text of law can change that for me."[15] In December 1940 and January 1941, Weil's stunning "The Iliad, or the Poem of Force" appeared in *Cahiers du Sud* under the pseudonym Emile Novis—a sort of anagram of Weil's name that she had taken up to avoid anti-Semitic feelings operative at the time, as well as to respect her parents' wish for discretion as the family waited to leave France.[16]

Weil's time in Marseilles featured what we now know as her signature combination of scholarship, activism, and theology. At the beginning of 1941, she started to study Sanskrit through René Daumal, who had become a scholar of India after being a surrealist.[17] She quickly got in touch with the poorest section of society: Indo-Chinese workers forcibly brought to France at the outbreak of the war to produce munitions.[18] Out of solidarity she attended their court trials.[19] She also became involved with other foreigners living there, many of whom were refugees fleeing fascism. Sensitive to the plight of refugees as well as others living in poverty, she avoided both food lines and the black market and lived on her ration coupons, often even giving some away.[20] She attended lectures at the Society of Philosophical Studies and, by the end of March 1941, a meeting of the Young Christian Workers.[21] It was through the poet Jean Tortel that she got in touch with the Resistance, which was under police surveillance. As a result, she was interrogated a number of times around April and May 1941. The police searched her family's home, including her room, which was filled with manuscripts. When the police called Weil to the police station after searching her home, she thought she might be arrested. Preparing for a long stay in custody, she brought a suitcase containing what she presumably considered to be the essentials: a few pieces of clothing and her copy of the *Iliad*.[22]

For many years Weil had wanted to understand the life of agricultural laborers, and she attempted to gain this understanding in spring 1941.[23] Through teacher Hélène Honnorat, Weil was introduced to the Dominican priest Joseph-Marie Perrin, who wrote to Weil and proposed a meeting on June 7, 1941.[24] It was through Perrin that she began to consider the question of baptism. Her interest in the Church remained strong. In the summer she intended to go to Carcassonne to hear Gregorian chant in the Abbey d'En-Calcat at Dourgne in the Tarn region, but she could not afford it.[25] In an effort to help Weil find a job as an agricultural laborer, Perrin turned to his friend Gustave Thibon, a Catholic writer who owned a farm in the Ardèche region. Thibon initially refused this proposal, but eventually he agreed to let her spend a few weeks in his house. They met at Avignon, then traveled together to Saint-Marcel, on August 7, 1941.

At Thibon's house Weil refused the room he offered, wanting to sleep outside. As a compromise she agreed to sleep at Thibon's wife's parents' house, which was half-ruined and situated on the banks of the Rhone river.[26] There, alongside a fireplace as well as rats and with a view of the Rhone valley and of a Romanesque church, she was very happy, sleeping on the ground in a sleeping bag with boards as a bed and pine needles for a mattress.[27] Such a life achieved what by then was her ideal combination of solitude, manual labor, and intermittent companionship.[28] She began working in the grape harvest sometime in mid-September in the village of Saint-Julien-de-Peyrolas, near Saint-Marcel in the Gard region.[29]

While idiosyncratic and characteristically extreme, her rejection of middle-class comforts was not a rejection of the world *per se*. On the contrary, it was her way of getting in touch with what she would come to call necessity. On September 11 she wrote to de Tarde that by approximating life as a peasant farmer she hoped "to have a serious contact with this world."[30] On September 10 or 11, she left for Poët with her parents. It was in Poët that she memorized the "Our Father" (in Greek) as part of a shared promise with Thibon that each would learn the prayer by heart.[31] She also read Saint John of the Cross in Spanish—Thibon had lent her the texts.[32] She left Poët on September 19 or 20 and stayed with the Thibons at Saint-Marcel before going to Saint-Julien, where a grape-grower (André Rieu) had agreed to take her on as a harvester. Once again—like her time in the factories—she was not treated like an anonymous laborer. Though she worked eight-hour days, she stayed and ate at the house of her employers.[33] On the first Sunday at this house, she asked for a missal and attended mass. The other Sundays she walked in the countryside, looked at the stars, and smoked cigarettes.[34]

On October 18 she wrote to Xavier Vallat, Commissioner of Jewish Affairs, claiming that she did not consider herself a Jew and thanking him for the "gift of poverty" she was experiencing as she harvested grapes.[35] She worked in the fields from September 22 to October 23.[36] She planned to work subsequently as a laborer for a truck gardener, but he decided to hire only people from his town, so she returned to Marseilles for the 1941–1942 winter.[37] In Marseilles she regularly attended mass on Sundays with Honnorat. She also led discussions on Greek thought at the local Dominican convent. Weil wrote to Thibon that though her baptism would please Father Perrin, she could not enter the Church simply for this reason. In fact, she continued, she felt more prepared to sacrifice her life for the Church than to join it.[38] The influence of her political and theological days exiled away from Paris can be seen in her 1941 writings.

MORAL REORIENTATION

Weil begins "Literature and Morals" with the claim that real evil is boring (LPW 145/EM I, 90).[39] We should understand this claim in light of her work in the factories, where time is oppressive in its repetition, in its monotony. Real evil, for Weil, is marked by necessity—it is "like gravity" (LPW 145/EM I, 91). With Plato, Weil sees necessity as running contrary to the good. It is the mark of finitude. It signals the impure, the conditional, the contingent, and the changing. But importantly, for Weil necessity itself does not carry any political connotations; it is simply woven into reality. As her Marxist biographer David McLellan comments on Weil's early writing, "What turned privilege into a force more brutal than that of natural necessity was the concomitant struggle for power."[40] So it would be incorrect to say that necessity is oppressive, as incorrect as it would be to say that the force of gravity itself is oppressive because it holds us firmly on the earth. No, necessity allows for order in the world. It is the reason we can have faith that each step we take will keep us on the ground. Oppression, Weil's keen eye discerns, emerges in a second stage, during the all-too-human struggle for power.

Oppressive power structures force humans to live out of balance with the forces of the world. As I discussed in chapter 1, Weil begins her "Factory Journal" with the epigraph she translated from the *Iliad*, "Much against your will, under pressure of harsh necessity." In doing so, she situated her year in the factories under not just the forces of the world, but under a turned-up, oppressive, or "harsh" necessity. And it is through this oppression that we might well turn against necessity ourselves, as the gig-economy taxi driver, Amazon worker, or person who delivers food via bicycle might start to hate the clock. In her beautiful reading of Weil, Joan Dargan comments on how in Weil's poem "Nécessité," the stars dance without cadence or time.[41] In other words, the stars have escaped the bounds of order, limit, and law. Such an escape is impossible for creatures on earth, and even more difficult under conditions of oppression. "Necessity erases each of us and we burn in silent anger," Dargan goes on, "the only way for us to imitate the stars."[42] Contrary to the argument that she was seeking to transcend her world, Weil's insight is to avoid holding on to an ideal, fabricated sense of otherworldly reality that moves beyond necessity. Instead, as Roberto Esposito has stressed, Weil theorizes freedom only and always through necessity.[43] Her concern, as we will see in continuing to read her 1941 writings, is about our orientation to good and evil amidst our daily and natural constraints.

Fictional evil, Weil goes on in "Literature and Morals," is protean: it takes on many forms and draws us in. It is seductive. Such a portrayal of evil aggrandizes it, removing people's focus away from the reality that evil is boring. Weil knew that evil was never in the immigrant of a different faith or ethnicity but in the oppressive systems within one's own country. And with such an insight in mind she was able to condemn the France of her time for living in "a fog of inverted values [*un brouillard où les valeurs sont renversées*]" (LPW 147/EM I, 92). She goes on to offer two ways that someone stumbling in a fog might reorient their values: first, through contact with reality itself; and second, through exposure to works of genius. By "genius" she has in mind Homer's *Iliad*, some plays of Shakespeare, and a few other canonical texts. So great is her frustration with her contemporaries that she toys with outlawing literature itself, concluding that it is saved only by the fact that if a country were to outlaw writing, it would not provide space for the few works of genius that could save it (LPW 148/EM I, 93).

In "Literature and Morals" Weil's central critique is of writers who have usurped priests as spiritual directors of a society. She blames less the writers and more the society as a whole. And more than a conservative call for priests to guide society, she adds that what she would really like to see is a society guided by saints. Lacking clear choices for saints in the present, she finds promise in past works of genius. How seriously are we to take these suggestions? The Marxist who is motivated by Weil's early writings likely feels lost at this point.

But Weil's Marxism lingers in this article. For instance, she makes a connection between writers' usurping the authority of priests and advertisements "for beauty cream promising a rich marriage to whoever uses it" (LPW 149/EM I, 94). It would be too much here to call Weil a paragon of cultural studies or a queer theorist taking marriage to task for the oppressive content that necessarily follows from a limited social form. Nevertheless, and as usual, her stark positions contain more than a kernel of insight. It is for observations such as this one—that advertisements have taken on the role of spiritual guidance in social life—that Weil can be read into contemporary debates on "political theology," meaning most broadly that she uses political language to talk about theology and theological language to talk about politics.[44] For there is a politics to the "spiritual usurpation" performed by the beauty cream advertisement (LPW 149/EM I, 94). It is that advertising orients the life of the "little village girls" not to find a healthy balance in the face of the necessity of the world but to pursue endlessly both a sense of beauty that time will always wear away and a class position ("*rich* marriage") that, through the exploitative production required to make such products and maintain some in luxurious positions, is *per se* hierarchical and oppressive.

In October 1940 and March 1941, *Cahiers du Sud* published two articles that tried to refute the claim—circulating in France at that time—that French writers had played a role in France's 1940 defeat at the hands of the Nazis. The argument was that the writers had chipped away at traditional French values and in the process lowered the strength of the country. Weil's 1941 letter to *Cahiers du Sud*, "The Responsibilities of Literature," not published until 1951, speaks to this context.

She begins that essay by saying that she does blame the writers for "the misfortune of our time" (LPW 151/EM I, 69). She then zooms out. The problem of her time, she says, is not the defeat of France but something larger. It has to do with the sense of value across the Western world. And the problem is not that people don't read. On the contrary, she acknowledges that people now read more than ever. She puts the problem in a description: "The essential characteristic of the first half of the twentieth century is the weakening and near disappearance of the concept of value" (LPW 152/EM I, 70). Sites where this decline in value can be seen include: places of production, where quantity is valued more than quality; the way skilled labor has been devalued; and perhaps especially in art, where Dadaism and Surrealism are catching on. Always attentive to the power of words, Weil also diagnoses the disappearance of what she calls value in language: words such as "spontaneity," "sincerity," and "richness"—words she sees as flattening and not truly related to the good—are thrown about. In philosophy, Henri Bergson's influential concept of "Life" lacks value. And in literature Marcel Proust is more concerned with beauty than value.

Weil's claim is not only that the aforementioned cultural forces have weakened the concept of value, but it is also that value has (nearly) disappeared. She is not, then, following Nietzsche, for instance, in tracing how values have shifted and are therefore contingent. While Weil's concept of necessity captures contingency and conditionality, she finds incorruptible values in a separate, time-out-of-mind plane. Combining Plato and Christian theology, she argues that the Good is contrary to necessity *spatially*, meaning it belongs to a different realm. Her discussion of morality is not a genealogy, but it is a critique of how the Western world has come to orient itself to the Good.

Pace some of Weil's critics, I suggest that perhaps she is not taking too much of a moralizing tone in these essays. Perhaps her conclusion of the essay is fair in stating that her expectation is not that writers become simple professors of morals but rather that "the 'moral reorientation' [« *redresse-ment* »] that certain people would like to impose would be much worse than the state of things that they are pretending to remedy" (LPW 154/EM I, 72). Her critique is different, then, from conservative morality programs today that impose a "right" sense of sexuality on others, to take one example. But she does want to hold artists accountable for expressing the human condition, even if she finally gives them some credit, claiming that "[t]hose who are currently putting the blame on famous writers are worth infinitely less than they" (LPW 154/EM I, 72). (We recall the start of the letter, where she was almost in pain at admitting that her position is "contrary to the view of this journal, and contrary to nearly everyone to whom I am sympathetic" [LPW 151/EM I, 69].) Her concluding call is poignant and demanding: "If our present suffering ever does lead to a moral reorientation, it will not be accomplished by slogans, but in silence and moral solitude, through pain, misery, terror, in the deepest part of each spirit [*le silence et la solitude morale, à travers les peines, les misères, les terreurs, dans le plus intime de chaque esprit*]" (LPW 154/EM I, 72).

On the one hand, there is something grim, almost macabre, about her conclusion. Terror? And does a reorientation have to be so painful? But on the other hand, in a world where we are constantly promised quick fixes in seven-step paths to happiness, there is something refreshing about the honesty with which Weil recognizes the depths of human life. In the remainder of this chapter, I think of Weil's concluding lines alongside the works of painter Mark Rothko, who also understood the need for solitude and silence in cultivating a reorientation of values. I bring Weil and Rothko together here for reasons borne out of personal experience. The most strongly I have felt Weil's call to live out a moral reorientation in silence, solitude, and pain was in the Rothko Chapel, an experience to which I will return below.

Writing on Rothko immediately runs into two constraints. First, much like Weil, he wrote a striking series of essays that he never published in his life, but that was collected and published posthumously by his family as *The Artist's Reality*. In that manuscript, he writes movingly about Plato, about how an artist depicts light, air, and space, and about the meaning of beauty itself. Because I am giving Weil the philosophical recognition I think she deserves by focusing mainly on her meant-for-publication writings, I will do the same for Rothko. The second limitation is that I am trained in neither art nor art history, so here I will approach Rothko through a phenomenological method, writing at times from my first-person perspective of his work. That said, by reading Weil alongside Rothko and in regard to how both challenge neoliberal understandings of the self, I speak to what, mentioning Rothko, the writer Ellen Handler Spitz calls the "open and unresolved question" of what is "the value of the heightened perceptual moments offered by the contemplation of works of art."[45] Part of the value, I will suggest, lies in how art opens the viewer to an awareness of the complexity of the self.

ROTHKO'S ATTUNEMENT

In the late 1920s, Mark Rothko worked as an illustrator and taught children. When he received an honorary doctorate from Yale in 1969, he said, "When I was a younger man, art was a lonely thing: no galleries, no collectors, no critics, no money."[46] Starting in 1936, still two years before he became a U.S. citizen, he made art for the Works Progress Administration, working for the WPA for three years. One element Weil and Rothko share in their work in the early 1940s is an understanding of the complexities of the self. Part of the work of art is to speak to these complexities, as opposed to simply forming an escape from inner life or contributing to bourgeois status. Familiar with poverty and life on the dole, Rothko would write with Adolph Gottlieb in a June 1943 op-ed in the *New York Times*, our art "must insult anyone who is spiritually attuned to interior decoration; pictures for the home; pictures for over the mantle."[47] In other words, how we approach art says something not just about our class status—whether we have a middle-class home and the disposable income to decorate it—but also about our spiritual orientation, what Rothko here calls "attunement" and what Weil calls "attention."

On an October 1943 radio program, Rothko dismissed the idea that modernity made life easier for humanity. "Those who think that the world today is more gentle and graceful than the primeval and predatory passions from which [ancient] myths spring," he states sharply, "are either not aware of reality or do not wish to see it in art."[48] And as for Weil, for Rothko reality is not a site of grace. On the contrary, it is a scene of turbulent, all-too-human emotions and struggles.

Rothko concluded a 1945 *New York Times* op-ed with a telling sentence: "If previous abstractions paralleled the scientific and objective preoccupations of our times, ours are finding a pictorial equivalent for man's new knowledge and consciousness of his more complex inner self."[49] His focus on the inner self notwithstanding, Rothko's art made a move Weil would criticize: his paintings, "like all myths, do not hesitate to combine shreds of reality with what is considered 'unreal' and insist upon the validity of the merger."[50] Weil's concern lies precisely in the merger between reality and the unreal. For the Weil of the early 1940s, Rothko's line about the unreal—"I quarrel with surrealist and abstract art only as one quarrels with his father and mother recognizing the inevitability and function of my roots"—would have put him out of contention for a work of "genius."[51] But Rothko's work, if not genius in Weil's sense, nevertheless resonates deeply with her concluding call in "Responsibilities of Literature," a point to which I will return below.

After the 1940s, Rothko would maintain his emphasis that art should speak to the complications of human emotional life. In a January 1952 interview with art historian and Museum of Modern Art curator William Seitz, Rothko states that he does not like to talk to painters. "They go to an exhibition, and remark on design, color, etc. Not pure human reactions."[52] It was the latter that Rothko sought. "I want pure response in terms of human need. Does the painting satisfy some human need?"[53] In a 1956 conversation, Rothko reiterated his project in terms of seeking a meaningful response. "I'm interested only in expressing basic human emotions—tragedy, ecstasy, doom and so on—and the fact that lots of people break down and cry when confronted with my pictures shows that I *communicate* those basic human emotions."[54] When he accepted an honorary doctorate from Yale in 1969 and commented, as aforementioned, that when he was young "art was a lonely thing: no galleries, no collections, no critics, no money," he added:

> Yet it was a golden time, for then we had nothing to lose and a vision to gain. Today it is not quite the same. It is a time of tons of verbiage, activity, and consumption. Which condition is better for the world at large I will not venture to discuss. But I do know that many who are driven to this life are desperately searching for those pockets of silence where they can root and grow. We must hope that they will find them.[55]

It is in these lines that we see most strongly Rothko's resonance with Weil. The normative thrust of his words is clear, belying his "I will not venture to discuss." When you paint for the Works Progress Administration, you have nothing to lose because you have no money. To argue that life is in fact richer without the attachments of fill-your-days business and sufficient disposable income for a lifestyle of consumption is not to glorify poverty. It is an honest retrospective.

Our time is a time of verbiage, activity, and consumption. With our phones on our nightstands or in our pockets, we forestall any hope to find pockets of silence. In our neoliberal context, especially amidst a pandemic, we are told to be resilient. It is not just Adidas commercials and Adam Grant's business books and interviews with Goldman Sachs that make this demand. The *New*

York Times and BBC run articles on resilience. The almost ambient message in our time is to spring back to pre-pandemic selves, to work harder, to be a self-starter. Any obstacle—including insurmountable student debt and a virus for which, at the time of writing this chapter, our species had not yet made a vaccine—can be hurdled, we are told. Just follow these seven steps. Wake up a little earlier. Track your movements with a smart watch. Get better.

The prescriptions of the resilience-mongers prove Marx correct when he stated that political economy is "the most moral of all the sciences."[56] "Self-denial, the denial of life and of all human needs," he goes on, "is its cardinal doctrine. The less you eat, drink, and read books; the less you go the theater, the dance hall, the public-house; the less you think, love, theorize, sing, paint, fence, etc. the more you *save*—the *greater* becomes your treasure which neither moths nor dust will devour—your *capital*."[57] To save all of your money, to delay your gratification constantly, Marx says, reduces not just life but everything that makes a life meaningful—your conversations with friends at the pub, the classical debates in philosophy you engage when you are not working—such that self-denial is a reduction of life itself. "The less you *are*," he says in his next line, "the more you *have*; the less you express your own life, the greater is your *alienated* life."[58]

From reading Rothko alongside Marx, we learn to avoid two ethical poles: the first is the active consumption Rothko rightly condemns. The second is the alienated self-deferral that Marx rightly condemns. Going to the pub or the theater every night can serve as a distraction that prevents us from sitting with our internal demons. But demanding of ourselves that we be resilient in the face of any political condition, that we spring back to a docile self that is eager to perform labor for our supervisors after any setback, that the best ethical and political response to facing insurmountable student debt or long-standing police violence in our communities is to work harder, to save more, to seize the day—such demands place the burden of change on the individual and not on the forces that exploit and oppress her. The sense of the self Weil and Rothko call us to attend to, especially when read through Marx, offers an ethical and political mode different from both consumption and resilience.

By the early 1940s, Weil was already concerned with how the distractions of modern life prevented an ethical orientation of attending to others. More than this, she had outlined how modern/colonial ways of life presuppose a simplistic notion of the self—little more than a worker by day and a consumer (of goods produced in oppressive conditions elsewhere) in the few hours when one is not working. She understood that living carefully goes far beyond taking a bath and allowing yourself a glass of good wine; it also looks like cultivating moments of deep contemplation of our complicated physical and emotional lives. Reading Weil as a feminist philosopher, Sophie

Bourgault writes, "Many care theorists could certainly appreciate Weil's conviction that there is such a thing as a basic and universal capacity to *feel* justice and injustice and that this capacity is partially rooted in our body, in the physical *experience* of pain."[59]

* * *

On the walls of the Rothko Chapel's welcome center, there are sayings about spirituality, human rights, and interfaith gathering. So often such broad calls for universal justice cannot go beyond superficial ethical points. But the mood of the Chapel itself, what it discloses in its call, is neither superficial nor general. It is profound and demanding, singling you out as you get lost in the images, thoughts, and feelings that the paintings provoke. I recall feeling overwhelmed in front of one of the darker paintings. It was as if the feeling was coming from the inside, asking me to face moments of despair in the solitude of the space.

In inaugurating the Chapel in 1971, its cofounder, Dominique de Menil, said about the paintings: "They will educate us to judge them. Every work of art establishes its own base for criticism. Every work of art creates the climate in which it can be understood."[60] Rothko rejected the social setting in which the paintings that became part of the Chapel were originally going to be presented. During the spring of 1958, architect Philip Johnson commissioned Rothko to make an ensemble for the Seagram Building in New York City. Initially Rothko accepted the offer, not knowing when he would next be asked to make a number of paintings to be put together. But before installation, he learned that his paintings were to serve as decoration in the restaurant of the Four Seasons hotel, so he refused to deliver them. In making such a refusal, not only did he lose money, but he also could have lost his last chance to create a mood that an ensemble of paintings allows. Menil and her husband offered him another chance.

Menil documents the history of the works, making clear why they could not serve as mere decoration: "As he worked on the Chapel . . . his colors became darker and darker, as if he were bringing us to the threshold of transcendence, the mystery of the cosmos, the tragic mystery of our perishable condition. The silence of God, the unbearable silence of God."[61] "Like all searches for the infinite," she continues about his process, "it emerged in darkness and silence."[62] Put differently, he "had the courage to paint almost nothing, and did it masterfully."[63] While Rothko's paintings across the chapel invoked for me what Weil, writing in her notebooks, would refer to as "the void" (*le vide*), Menil qualifies her reading of the darkness of the paintings. "Indeed it is the night," she says, "but not quite. Even in the dim light, purplish color slowly emerges from the darkness . . . it is predawn."[64]

The Marxist writer and art historian John Berger also argues that Rothko's paintings invoke a new beginning. "Rothko's art," he states, "is unique in the way that it treats immigration."[65] "Other artists were more nostalgic, more personal, more adventurous, more agonized," Berger says, "but nobody else—or so it seems to me—saw how the drama of emigration could turn the language of painting inside out."[66] Berger means that previous painting "from the paleolithic caves to modern abstraction" considered "the visible as found in the existent visible world."[67] Rothko's paintings propose the opposite; they regard "colours or light *awaiting* the creation of the visible world."[68] If his paintings reference something, they point to "the very first act of Creation"—they are "a quest on canvas for the Beginning, the Origin."[69] If Berger is right, then Rothko's paintings resonate with Weil's philosophy because of their shared stress not only on the ethics of waiting, of attention, but also on the politics of what is not yet, but what we can hear by listening to the world for its internal contradictions. Berger writes, "Rothko turned painting inside out because the colors he so laboriously created are waiting to depict things which do not yet exist."[70] This is "an emigrant art" because it is "[s]eeking, as only emigrants do, the unfindable place of origin, the moment before everything began."[71]

The ethical and political question is: How does this confrontation with pain through contemplating Rothko's paintings, paintings that invoke (at least for me) a sense of the void, contribute to a moral reorientation? Writing in a mode in which historical materialists will be more comfortable, Berger says elsewhere, "Painting and sculpture are clearly not the most suitable means for putting pressure on the government to nationalize the land."[72] Nevertheless, in engaging such artwork there is an occurrence "less direct and more comprehensive."[73] "After we have responded to a work of art, we leave it, carrying away in our consciousness something which we didn't have before."[74] In my view, the Rothko Chapel exemplifies not a work of genius leading us to be in touch with a different plane but a work of art that asks us to consider the continuities and discontinuities in ourselves—to carry with us a newfound plurality in our understanding of ourselves. The work that these paintings accomplish, what they give us which we didn't have before, is an honest portrait of interior life so often denied in neoliberal times.

THE ETHICS AND POLITICS OF SELF-PLURALITY

What Weil understood and teaches is that an acknowledgment of our own complications, struggles, ambiguities, and pains can cause us to shift how we relate to others. It is this acknowledgment that neoliberalism tries to overcome or repress instead of accept. Through an insistence on self-growth, often aided by a new purchase, neoliberal ethics reject the claim that we are fundamentally beings in tension. We are supposed to wear an electronic bracelet to know ourselves better and feel more fit, attractive, and productive—indeed often to *link* how attractive we are to how productive we are. We can *will* ourselves to a better future. Weil would critique this claim not just on Marxist grounds—a more productive worker remains alienated and, lacking knowledge of production, unfree—but also on anthropological grounds. That is, her understanding of the human, of the self, offers an alternative claim: to be human is to confront the void. The void is emptiness. The confrontation involves searching. In anxiety and discomfort, we tend to imagine some (false) stability: a nation that is great, a successful self, and even, she says, a warm cup of tea. Weil calls these images "compensation" in the face of a cold world (GG 17/25). To suspend the idols we create to fill the ultimate emptiness of experience is the beginning of an ethics, of an ethical turn. For this suspension of our imagination allows us to attend to the world in its fullness and reality, as opposed to posing quickly some thing as compensation. In a moment where we suspend our projections, we create the conditions to begin to attend to needs of others, and in that rare attention to others—and not to making ourselves more attractive, successful, secure, or stable—the possibility for a new society emerges. This is a social or political example of how for Weil "attention is creative [*attention est créatrice*]" (WG 52/99), here creative of a new international consciousness seen for instance in the politics of refusal, refusing the compensations of the face cream, the tea, or another product made in near-slavery conditions through a global division of labor.[75]

There has been much ink spilled over Weil's ethics of attention and decreation. Instead of reading more of her specific notebook entries and letters, I want to suggest something else, namely, that Weil's notebooks and letters *as a whole* provide an example of an individual—not a saint or a genius but a human, all-too-human philosopher—working "in silence and moral solitude, through pain, misery, terror, in the deepest part of [her] spirit" (LPW 154/EM I, 72). Read this way, Weil is an exemplary political philosopher, a model to follow, not just because in her we find an example of trying to act against the injustices of the empire in which she lives but also because she tarries with internal conflicts instead of writing them off as unproductive limitations to realizing a whole, flourishing, easy, unencumbered self—an ideal that is itself a compensation for the pain that is modern human life.

Writing about desire, philosopher and travel writer Alphonso Lingis describes a possibility for a relationship to the self beyond exclusion or repression. To make a division, to set up a wall between parts of ourselves

> may function to maintain a nonconfrontational coexistence of different sectors of oneself. One may value an affable relationship with the beast within oneself.

One may not want to penetrate behind that wall, not out of horror and fear of what lies behind, but because one may choose to be astonished at the strange lusts contained within oneself. One may want the enigmas and want the discomfiture within oneself.[76]

A mark of the success of this chapter is whether I open any room for thinking of Weil as a moral philosopher who attended to the enigmas and discomfitures within herself. (Again, Blanchot's "I do not see why Simone Weil alone would be disqualified as a thinker because she accepted within herself as legitimate the inevitable opposition of thoughts" echoes in my mind.[77]) A reading of her work—her essays' calls for spiritual solitude as well as her notebook entries on denying oneself—that remains underdeveloped is one that considers her writing as making room for, allowing, perhaps even appreciating what Lingis calls "the discomfiture within oneself." Seen through this lens, Weil's writing about the pain and terror that a person might feel starts to seem less as another part of her saintly suffering and more an honest reflection on the modern/colonial psychological conditions: the burden of living through repeated economic and environmental crises amidst calls to be resilient, calls that do not acknowledge the terror of living in that experience.

But is there a politics to understanding the self as plural and thus allowing it space to dwell in its multiplicities? It is arguable that neoliberalism also understands the self as divided and plural, and then suggests a new purchase or a "new you" as the way to (temporarily) overcome that former self. This new self then needs to be overcome again through yet another act of consumption. If both the neoliberal consumerist understanding and Weil's understanding of the self is similar in this way, then how are they different? I suggest the difference lies in how Weil's response to internal division was not consumption or the perpetual drive for improvement but to understand that division as partially coming from the demands of others, and in turn responding to those demands. If Weil, as I have read her against the grain here, gives us a hint at the politics of a conflicted self, then we also see the ethical importance of art such as Rothko's. Such art, in inviting contemplation of the deepest needs and urgencies of oneself, interrupts and disrupts a coherent sense of oneself, not to overcome it perpetually but to learn how that self is connected to others. One strong piece of evidence for my suggestion that we read Weil's personal writings as a consideration of the strangeness within herself, in a way that links her to others, is that her *praxis* in Marseilles carried out what is possible perhaps only following a discovery of our own abysses, namely, a truly just orientation to, or mode of action with, foreigners.[78] In Weil's terms, we might call this mode love, as when she asks in a 1937 letter: "Is there a nation founded on love? I mean on the love of foreigners?"[79]

In the next chapter, I will turn to Weil's critique of the language of rights, a critique she develops in part because rights rely on the power of the immigrant-excluding nation.

NOTES

1. Jessica Whyte, *The Morals of the Market: Human Rights and the Rise of Neoliberalism* (New York: Verso, 2019), 232.

2. Ibid.

3. Ibid. Another question also inspired this chapter: "And what do human beings become when dispossessed, not of their things nor even of their house, but of what links them to interiority?" (Jacques Derrida and Anne Dufourmantelle, *Of Hospitality* [Stanford: Stanford University Press, 2000], 130).

4. See Pétrement, *Simone Weil*, 450.

5. *Cahiers du Sud* was the most important literary magazine in the free zone. Walter Benjamin met the editor of *Cahiers du Sud*, Jean Ballard, in 1928; Benjamin's "Hashish in Marseilles" was published in the January 1935 issue. In November 1938 Benjamin attended a banquet for contributors to *Cahiers du Sud* at the brasserie L'Alsacienne, where he was among Paul Valéry, Jean Wahl, and others (see Howard Eiland and Michael W. Jennings, *Walter Benjamin: A Critical Life* [Cambridge, MA: Belknap Press of Harvard University Press, 2016], 621).

6. Pétrement, *Simone Weil*, 378. The Nazis arrived in Paris on June 14.

7. Pétrement, *Simone Weil*, 379.

8. Ibid., 382.

9. Ibid., 382–83.

10. Ibid., 382.

11. Ibid., 382, 384.

12. Ibid., 385.

13. Ibid., 389.

14. Ibid., 390.

15. Ibid., 392. Despite the June 2, 1941, decree that all Jews in the free zone must register as Jewish, Weil did not register (ibid., 421). In September 1940 she admitted to the political usefulness of casting Jews as scapegoats (Dargan, *Simone Weil*, 9).

16. Dargan, *Simone Weil*, 12.

17. Pétrement, *Simone Weil*, 394.

18. McLellan, *Utopian Pessimist*, 163.

19. For an extended treatment of Weil's time as a refugee in Marseilles, see Lyndsey Stonebridge, "Simone Weil's Uprooted" in *Placeless People: Writing, Rights, and Refugees* (New York: Oxford, 2018), 96–118.

20. Pétrement, *Simone Weil*, 398. Weil had written to André in early March 1941 that she would rather be the object of persecution than of philanthropy (ibid., 396). Perhaps stetching this line, we could read it as yet another example of the agency of the persecuted that can be understood not as self-hatred but as an anti-colonial critique that understands the paternalism and colonialism of philanthropy.

21. Ibid., 403; McLellan, *Utopian Pessimist*, 166.

22. Pétrement, *Simone Weil*, 409.

23. In a letter to Gilbert Kahn on the day before she left for Saint-Marcel to begin her work as "more or less a farm girl," she wrote, "I regard physical work as a purification—but a purification on the order of suffering and humiliation. One can also find in it, in its very depths, instants of profound, nourishing joy that cannot be equaled elsewhere" (Pétrement, *Simone Weil*, 423).

24. Perrin lived at the Dominican house on rue Edmond Rostand (McLellan, *Utopian Pessimist*, 170).

25. Pétrement, *Simone Weil*, 413.

26. Ibid., 425.

27. Ibid., 426.

28. McLellan, *Utopian Pessimist*, 174.

29. Pétrement, *Simone Weil*, 431.

30. Ibid., 434.

31. This is likely the first time Weil prayed (McLellan, *Utopian Pessimist*, 176). Thus, we see prayer beginning in relation and friendship. McLellan attributes Weil's lack of praying before to her fear of autosuggestion—imagination and idolatry.

32. McLellan, *Utopian Pessimist*, 176.

33. Pétrement, *Simone Weil*, 440.

34. McLellan, *Utopian Pessimist*, 177.

35. Pétrement, *Simone Weil*, 443–44.

36. Ibid., 444.

37. Ibid., 445.

38. Ibid., 447.

39. I could not find the French versions of these essays through the digital library of Les Classiques des sciences sociales, so I cite the page numbers of the physical copy of Weil's *Écrits de Marseille*, from tome IV, volume I, of her *Oeuvres Complètes.*

40. McLellan, *Utopian Pessimist*, 83.

41. Dargan, *Simone Weil*, 91.

42. Ibid., 93.

43. Esposito, *Origin*, 10.

44. See Lloyd, *The Problem with Grace*, (Stanford: Stanford University Press, 2011), 2.

45. Ellen Handler Spitz, *Art and Psyche: A Study in Psychoanalysis and Aesthetics* (New Haven, CT: Yale University Press, 1985), 20.

46. Mark Rothko, *Writings on Art* (New Haven, CT: Yale University Press, 2006), 157.

47. Ibid., 36.

48. Ibid., 39–40.

49. Ibid., 46.

50. Ibid.

51. Ibid., 45.

52. Ibid., 78.

53. Ibid.

54. Ibid., 117.

55. Ibid., 157.

56. Karl Marx, *The Economic and Philosophic Manuscripts of 1844*, trans. Martin Milligan (New York: Prometheus Books, 1988), 118.

57. Ibid., 119.

58. Ibid.

59. Bourgault, "Beyond," 6.

60. Dominique de Menil, *The Rothko Chapel: Writings on Art and the Threshold of the Divine* (New Haven, CT: Yale University Press, 2010), 17.

61. Ibid., 22.

62. Ibid., 37.

63. Ibid., 27.

64. Ibid., 36.

65. John Berger, *Portraits* (New York: Verso, 2017), 329.

66. Ibid., 330.

67. Ibid.

68. Ibid.

69. Ibid.

70. Ibid.

71. Ibid.

72. John Berger, *Landscapes: John Berger on Art* (New York: Verso, 2016), 96.

73. Ibid.

74. Ibid.

75. Of course, Weil herself maintained some attachments, in particular to cigarettes. Her friends write, "Of all the things belonging to material life, tobacco was the only one which she was almost certain to accept" (Perrin and Thibon, *Simone Weil*, 114).

76. Alphonso Lingis, *Abuses* (Berkeley: University of California Press, 1994), 128.

77. Blanchot, *Infinite Conversation*, 106.

78. In *Strangers to Ourselves*, philosopher and psychoanalyst Julia Kristeva argues that political justice for foreigners begins with an examination and understanding of the foreigner within ourselves. "By recognizing him within ourselves," she writes, "we are spared detesting him in himself" (Julia Kristeva, *Strangers to Ourselves*, trans. Leon S. Roudiez [New York: Columbia University Press, 1991], 1). This recognition is a start. It begins "with the moment when the citizen-individual ceases to consider himself as unitary and glorious but discovers his incoherences and abysses, in short his 'strangeness'" (ibid., 2). From this beginning, the question is no longer "that of welcoming the foreigner within a system that obliterates him but of promoting the togetherness of those foreigners that we all recognize ourselves to be" (ibid., 2–3). Kristeva's inquiry seeks a mode of living without others "without ostracism but also without leveling" (ibid., 2).

79. See Pétrement, *Simone Weil*, 290.

Chapter 4

Critique of Human Rights

Living in exile in London, where she worked with the Free French, Simone Weil wrote the essay "Human Personality" sometime between the winter of 1942 and the spring of 1943, the final year of her life. Exiled for her Jewish background, for what she was and not what she did (in Hannah Arendt's terms), Weil had reason to be skeptical toward the promises of a nation-state, even and especially her own. Yet she was also hopeful for the new political organization that could emerge at the end of France's occupation. In this chapter, I focus on Weil's critique of rights with respect to neoliberal-ism. While the Free French tasked Weil with writing about a concrete issue, such as trade-union problems, in "Human Personality" she articulated three concerns about rights vis-à-vis power: (1) rights rely on force and therefore can be used to advance the agenda of the powerful; (2) rights are suited to disguise power; and (3) rights inhibit solidarity in organizing against power.

Recent scholarship, especially that critical of a neoliberal turn in rights discourse, has emphasized all three of these concerns about the history and language of human rights. In regard to Weil's first concern, the connection between rights and force, historian Elizabeth Borgwardt has shown how the institutions of the international human rights regime serve U.S. national security and economic interests even when they claim to advance global priorities.[1] In regard to Weil's second concern, that the language of rights dresses domination in a cloak of philanthropy, philosopher Jessica Whyte has demonstrated that "human rights discourses have been mobilized in defence of wealth and power in the period of neoliberal hegemony."[2] Legal theorist Jayan Nayar adds, "We are all Human Rights-subjects now, subject to naming and emplacing of subject-beingness. As such may we be *contained* with rights and obligations if we remain docile, obedient and worthy, but *abandoned* (even banned) to abject rightlessness if we are deemed not so."[3] And historian Samuel Moyn notes, "Even those who retain an investment in human rights cannot treat them as an unquestionable good," because "the America that once seemed to many enthusiasts to be the prospective servant of universality abroad all too quickly became the America pursuing low-minded imperial ambitions in high-minded humanitarian tones."[4] "The effect on human rights as a public language and political cause," Moyn concludes, "has been staggering, and it is not yet clear whether they can recover."[5] In regard to Weil's third concern, that the language of rights can mitigate mobilization, writing against the taken-for-granted good of *inclusion* in a common humanity, social theorist Ayça Çubukçu has criticized "the endorsement of humane kinds of violence by human rights advocates," reminding her readers that "benevolence and violence can be mutually dependent."[6] "[T]he ideal of humanity and its conceptual and practical history," Çubukçu adds, "have always involved the withdrawal of solidarity and the denial of equality to certain human beings whose humanity, as membership in a species, was nevertheless granted."[7] How, then, do Weil's contributions prefigure, contribute to, or end up as limited when compared to these recent critiques?

My argument below is that from placing Weil in dialogue with the above theorists, justice-oriented actors gain two considerations: first, a methodological push to attend to how ethical concepts function in practice as well as a related courage, when necessary, to invent new terms and forms; and second, a compassionate call to link practice to theory in a way that inspires solidarity with those we claim to defend in our writing. This chapter proceeds in three parts: I read Weil's critique of the human person (*personne humaine*) presented by philosophers of Personalism, a conception of the person that would be foundational for human rights. I then expand on her aforementioned threefold critique of rights. I conclude by making explicit what Weil offers human rights theory and practice today. Throughout my commentary on her essay "Human Personality," I will keep in mind the words she placed as the title of her original Manuscript: "Collectivity. Person. Impersonal. Right. Justice."

RIGHTS AND COLLECTIVITY

In "Human Personality" Weil compares any collectivity to the "great beast" Plato describes in his *Republic*. Her specific concern is with the language of the collectivity, which uses words such as "rights" and "democracy."

> The concept of rights is linked to that of sharing out, of exchange, of quantity. It has something of the commercial to it. It evokes legal proceedings and pleadings. Rights are always asserted in a tone of contention; and when this tone is adopted, force is not far behind to back it up, otherwise, it would be ridiculous. (LPW 113)

La notion de droit est liée à celle de partage, d'échange, de quantité. Elle a quelque chose de commercial. Elle évoque par elle-même le procès, la plaidoirie. Le droit ne se soutient que sur un ton de revendication; et quand ce ton est adopté, c'est que la force n'est pas loin, derrière lui, pour le confirmer, ou sans cela il est ridicule. (EL 22)

A market logic marks rights claims. On this account, such claims are fit for argumentation, not for a pursuit of justice. Most problematically for this pursuit, rights claims need to be enforced; in other words, for Weil, rights claims are inherently tied to violence, including and especially state violence. For these reasons, political scientist Helen Kinsella reads Weil as describing rights claims as "an illusion"; they "inure one from the true suffering of the other."[8] "There are a number of notions, all in the same category," Weil goes on, "that are in themselves entirely foreign to the supernatural and are, however, a bit above brute force. They are all relative to the mores of the beast of the collective, to use the language of Plato . . . The notions of rights, of the personal, of democracy, are all in this category" (LPW 113/EL 22).

These notions are slightly better for guiding social life than force, but only slightly, because they depend on such force. We can be suspicious of calls to "democracy," for instance, insofar as that democracy relies on police enforcement in the background (or, really, in the foreground). Through its abstract language, always tied to the whims of the beast, the collectivity hides the violence it commits. And yet there is a kind of seduction by the collectivity. This is Weil's central concern. "[T]he greater danger is not the tendency of the collective to curb the personal, but the tendency of the personal to throw itself into, to drown itself in the collective. Or perhaps the first danger is only the apparent and deceitful aspect of the second" (LPW 111/EL 19). It is not simply that one participates in a collectivity and one feels stifled. More precisely, one first feels called by the collective in some way, such that one throws oneself into it. Why?

Those who throw themselves into a collectivity, Weil writes, experience "not an authentic sense of the sacred, but a false imitation of it produced by the collective" (LPW 111/EL 19). "If they experience it through their own person," she goes on "this is because it participates in the collective prestige through the social consideration of which it finds itself to be the site . . . In a human being, the personal is a thing in distress, it is cold, it runs about looking for a refuge and for warmth" (LPW 111/EL 20). She ultimately presents a political anthropology or, perhaps more precisely, a political psychology. The individual—and this is more clear in the French *personne*, which can mean "no one" and which is the key term of the opening of the essay in the French—seeks something greater than itself, something in which it can be safe. Weil does not deny this impulse. Indeed, at this point in her life, she endorses an orientation to what she calls in the above quotation "an authentic sense of the sacred." Her more precise concern is that the collective produces idols, a "false imitation."

Idolatry notwithstanding, it is worth noting that participation in prestigious collectivities often quite literally provides warmth: when one is co-opted into institutional structures, one gains financial and material rewards. Weil saw easy accommodation to prestigious structures as morally bankrupt.[9] In sum, what we gain from her text is an emphasis on the importance of the language that a collectivity uses and an explanation for the staying power of the collectivity, namely, how it speaks to an anthropological need. The more specific critique Weil makes in the essay is of Personalism, and in particular of its version of human rights.

"Human Personality" can be read as a position paper against founding a polity on rights-based doctrines. Edward Andrew reads the essay in keeping with a Marxist critique of rights: "For Weil, the rights-based society is founded on the politics of property," and in this context "the holdings of one powerful group are traded off in exchange for mutual renunciation (or compromise) of the holdings of other powerful groups."[10] Thus, in regard to economics, rights contribute to commercializing or commodifying all aspects of life. In regard to politics, rights presuppose a society based on private property, and in this way reinforce existing power relations. And in regard to ethics, rights allow the individual to make choices; they do not produce fair or equitable choices. Andrew writes: "Rights, like properties," Andrew explains following Weil, "function to protect choices or secure options; unlike obligations, rights do not function to guide conduct."[11] On this account, rights make attending to the afflicted one option among others. Andrew writes: "Rights are connected to power while obligations are allied to love. We make claims *against* others; we have obligations *to* others."[12] On Andrew's reading, in taking on rights discourse for allowing unjust choices, Weil criticizes "the moral core of liberalism."[13] In my view, Andrew is correct to highlight Weil's critique of rights as a critique of liberalism—and to stress that Weil's critique is a conservative one with which many of us are uncomfortable. She will go on, for instance, to endorse government censorship, so concerned with the truth is she. What separates my reading of Weil's critique of rights from Andrew's is not so much how we read Weil as it is how we position that reading: for Andrew, it is with respect to liberalism; for me, it is with respect to neoliberalism. Weil's direct target was neither. Instead, she was concerned with the rise of Personalism in her time.

CRITIQUE OF PERSONALISM

Personalism makes a distinction between the individual and the person: whereas the *individual* is part of a larger social whole, the *person* is itself a whole. With the dignity of the person in mind, Personalist philosophers argued that the person should be treated as an end in itself. As an individual, one should contribute to the social order of which one is a part, but as a person, one should not in any way be placed under, or subordinated to, that social order.

In important ways Personalism redefined the person from its traditional meaning. "Person" is a Roman category both theatrical and juridical. *Persona* names both the mask of an actor and the ability of an individual to be represented before the law.[14] Unlike how we hear "personality" today, then, the term has its origins not in individualized particularity or difference but as a relation to sameness—not as a way one is distinct from one's social and political order but precisely as how one fits into that order. The Roman person realized its full potential by participation as a citizen. Personalists, then, departed from this meaning in developing their vocabulary: to say that "person" signifies something beyond the individual, and that the person is essentially a whole that should limit the social order, is to work against its Roman conceptualization, in which the person was an entity with obligations to, and that realized itself precisely within, the social order.[15]

For Jacques Maritain, the most influential philosopher of Personalism regarding human rights, the end of each person is to achieve spiritual perfection. Human rights provide the means to achieve that perfection. On his account, human rights are based in natural rights—they are antecedent to society and inalienable. As he states in his 1942 *Natural Law and Human Rights*, "[A] revival of natural law implies a broad set of pre-political human rights."[16] In at least one way, then, Personalism resonates with neoliberalism: namely, both claim that the good lies in a purportedly nonpolitical sphere. But the intention of Personalism was to steer a middle course between liberalism and communism, avoiding individualism, on the one hand, and a perceived lack of spiritual and moral values, on the other. Personalism's conception of the human person is important for the purposes of this chapter not just because it was Weil's object of criticism in "Human Personality" but because, Moyn explains, it was "the conceptual means through which Continental Europe initially incorporated human rights—and, indeed, became the homeland of the notion for several decades."[17] In investigating human rights discourse today, then, we would do well to ask: How does the inheritance from Personalism condition and limit practices around human rights today? Weil's critique is a point of departure.

Weil approached her critique of rights through a critique of the *personne* of Personalism. To base moral thought on the concept of the person was an error of vocabulary, for Weil, and "wherever there is a grave error in vocabulary, it is hard to avoid grave errors in thought" (LPW 104/EL 11). By her lights, the "person" is not what is sacred about the human. For this reason, the language of the person does not suffice for what the philosophers of Personalism want the concept to do.

Her argument begins by noting that "human personality" (*la personne humaine*) cannot be defined. In addition to a definitional problem, there is also a practical problem. She illustrates the latter through an example: one could stab the eyes of another but not thereby injure another's human personality. So she asks, "What is it that keeps me from poking out his eyes, if I am allowed to do so [*si j'en ai la licence*], and might even find it amusing?" (LPW 104/EL 12). What *would* prevent her, she says in an answer to her own question, "is the knowledge that if someone were to poke out his eyes that it would be his soul that was lacerated by the thought that someone had done evil to him" (LPW 105/EL 13). What is sacred in a human is not a personality, for Weil, but the "something that goes on expecting, from infancy to the grave, that good and not evil will be done to us, despite the experience of crimes committed, suffered, and observed" (LPW 105/EL 13). We might call this *the expectation of good*. The expectation of good is sacred because it is linked, she claims in a Platonic register, to "the good" (*le bien*) (LPW 105/EL 13).

Weil's critique of the ordinary language of "person"—that it does not function practically to stay violence—is especially important for considerations of rights because of the status of ordinary language in law, wherein the everyday usage of a term remains operative. As U.S. Supreme Court Chief Justice Berger noted in 1979 in *Perrin v. United States*, "A fundamental canon of statutory construction is that, unless otherwise defined, words will be interpreted as taking their ordinary, contemporary, common meaning."[18] For the Personalists to say that they were simply giving "person" a meaning different from its everyday usage, then, is to take away from the applicability of the concept in law.

Weil's critique of the person is helpful because it reminds us that *a concept itself* cannot prevent harmful action. Here an interlocutor might reply: Can *any* concept do this kind of practical work? Not exactly—or not by itself. But concepts serve to guide our practices. How we frame the world shapes our actions in it. An interlocutor might also note that the *vocabulary* of human rights is not precisely that of Personalism. While the language of human rights is that of the human and not of the person (and therefore this language cannot be accused of *the same* error of vocabulary of Personalism), much human rights language relies on a natural rights argument akin to that of Personalism. The framing of the 2016 protests at Standing Rock as a human rights struggle around water, for instance, relied on an implicit argument that all humans have a right to water as part of a right to life. Further, at the borders of the United States and on Indigenous land in Nicaragua and Brazil, we see that the humanity of some certainly does not prevent others from "sheltering" them in inhumane conditions or taking their land by force. I will return to this critique of human rights below.

For now, we might pose again Weil's question concerning ethics: What is it, precisely, that prevents one from harming another when one is able to and desires to—when one has a sense of license? This is one of the most fundamental questions in the history of ethical and political theory, with answers ranging from the early historian Thucydides's realistic account of the Melian Dialogue—that the strong do what they will and the weak do what they must—to philosopher Emmanuel Levinas's attempt, in the wake of the Holocaust, to present "the face" as a check on violence. Today, the language of "human rights violations," as a shorthand for a variety of violent actions, presupposes that human rights are an entity themselves that should be respected; they are a concept invoked to do real ethical work. Weil extended her critique of Personalism to a critique of rights. What can we learn from this extension? What does it bring into relief regarding the limitations of human rights as an ethical concept?

CRITIQUE OF RIGHTS

As we saw above, for Weil the essence and appearance of rights resonate with bargain and commerce. Rights are a way of making claims, and the tone of those claims is one of imbalance, strife, debate—contention. But how serious of a problem is it, for claims to rights, that they rely on force? Can we even grant Weil's point?

Political rights are traditionally understood as a *check* on power. Rights claims are made on the state, delimiting its sphere of control: the civil and political rights of speech and assembly are examples here. Other kinds of rights, however, are demands on power to provide something. Social and economic rights obligate the state to do something: to meet a need of healthcare or education, say. More recently, some have articulated collective rights, such as the right to self-determination or the right of an ethnic minority to enjoy its own culture. These rights are also a check on power, often attempting to avoid the standardizing imposition of a dominant state or majority therein. Neoliberals support (some) political rights but see a contradiction between political and economic rights, worrying that the freedom of many (a negative freedom, such as freedom from state involvement) will be lessened if, for example, the state provides healthcare for all (a positive freedom). Leftists often make the opposite point, arguing that a meaningful sense of freedom requires (positing) health, education, and so on—and therefore requires state involvement. Different evaluations of positive and negative freedom underlie which rights are demanded and prioritized.

Weil's specific claim is not that rights depend on force. It is that a tone of contention must rely on force. Contention suggests conflict. The "stronger" (in force if certainly not in moral qualities) of the two sides will win. We have seen Weil's point being proven correct as the strongest countries—where strength is defined in terms of military might and GDP—maintain their sovereignty by not signing treaties that would subject them to the judgment of international courts. The United States can laugh at small countries' claims to human rights because the United States is an imperial power with an excessive military force. Why become a state party to the Rome Statute when you are not compelled to? This impunity of powerful countries suggests that Weil is correct about rights relying on force among states.

It is also the case that rights rely on force within states. When citizens of the United States assert that "Water is Life" or "Black Lives Matter," they are making a claim on the state, namely, and respectively, that the state is denying life by contaminating water (through creating the dispossessive conditions for, allowing, and subsidizing a pipeline) and that the state is not counting the lives of Black people as valuable lives given its use of police force. In the cases of Standing Rock and Ferguson, these assertions are not attended to. Rather, the state doubles down on its force—we can think of the drones around Standing Rock or the way the Department of Homeland Security monitors the social media of Black Lives Matter. This kind of surveillance is another way that the powerful ridicules rights claims.

In developing her critique of rights, Weil makes a further, fascinating claim, "The Romans, who understood, like Hitler, that force is not fully effective unless it is dressed in certain ideas, employed the concept of rights in this way" (LPW 114/EL 23). This is to say that power wears clothes, and doing so makes it more efficacious. Here we can think of how the U.S. invasion of Iraq was justified in terms of democracy and human rights. What is especially worth thinking about is why the idea of rights is *suited* to power. (The play on the clothing here makes this a very nice translation: we even have the term "power suits" to describe what bankers, lawyers, and other powerful professionals wear to work on a daily basis.)

Recent commentators, challenging a neoliberal turn in human rights discourse, have explained that rights are suited to power because the language of human rights almost always calls for a minimal instead of a maximal demand, reform instead of political transformation. Samuel Moyn and Jessica Whyte have observed a kind of political minimalism in regard to human rights: human rights movements are different from more demanding movements, such as movements for decolonization, in part because whereas the latter demanded collective independence, the former often focuses on single "bad actors." For instance, Amnesty International has historically drawn international focus to corrupt leaders but generally avoided more systematic or institutional criticisms. If the focus can stay on rights, then the contests can stay in the present institutions. Lawyers can be called. Struggle is muted—or at least transmuted to the institutional frameworks of the state. Moyn explains this critical minimalism in terms of a shift from politics to morals:

> In 1968, human rights were in crisis, because their partisans had not found a way to ally themselves with an exploding wave of popular movements. But they hit on a way to do so only amid the exhaustion of utopian energies of the era and through a move from politics to morality. It was the crucial imaginative transformation that mattered. In the long view, what the substitution of moral for political utopianism meant is that human rights came to the world as its partisans abjured the maximalism that had once lent utopias glamor—especially utopias that required profound transformation, or even revolution and violence.[19]

Whyte has added that the drafters of the Universal Declaration "sought to detach social and economic rights from political challenges to the exploitation of labour, the existing division of labour and the reproductive role of the nuclear family, and transform them into minimalist guarantees for the most needy."[20] She has also demonstrated how the very way that human rights organizations problematize global violence sets the tensions so as to move away from radical politics and toward state control. "[I]n conceptualising the *problem* as politics and the *solution* as law," she explains, "the human rights NGOs bolstered the neoliberal dichotomy between violent politics and peaceful markets, secured by constitutional restrictions."[21] Weil's note that rights are suited to power is a useful shorthand to explain the political minimalism of human rights that these recent contributions have underscored.

Weil's third claim in her critique of rights is that rights claims inhibit charity. Here she moves to a religious register slightly different from her initial political criticisms. But her religious sensibility is thoroughly interlaced with the politics of solidarity she has in mind and exemplified when she was writing this essay. "Rights," she argues, "do not have any direct link with love" (LPW 115/EL 24). "The concept of rights, put at the center of social conflicts, makes any nuance of charity impossible there on both sides" (LPW 115/EL 24). Charity for Weil, following Augustine's *caritas*, is a form of fellowship. It thus implies a social relation and connection, what for late Weil are creaturely relations that preexist legal mediation. Whereas corporate and humanitarian philanthropy involves a distanced do(mi)nation, the implication of fellowship in charity involves a concrete commitment, a grounded *praxis*. In contexts of social conflict, Weil is saying, one should be able to ask another, "What are you going through? [*Quel est ton tourment*?]" (WG 36/74). The courtroom is not the place for this—and at their most effective, rights claims, at least traditionally understood, will bring us to the courtroom.[22]

Weil's example of injustice in "Human Personality" is the poor person "stammering before a judge who is making clever jokes in elegant language" (LPW 106/EL 14). Part of her point is that those who have suffered injustice are not trained in making claims about their affliction in a way legible to the institutions Western societies have created to mete out justice. What Weil says she is after is the same thing that human rights advocates and humanitarians say they are after: a response to the affliction of the present—social, psychological, material, and spiritual suffering. But her first move is different from many of those advocates and aid workers. Whereas reformers adopt the terms of the present, radicals start from a position of doubt, a hesitation before and rejection of present institutions. The political party, Weil diagnoses in "Human Personality" as well as in the contemporaneous *On the Abolition of All Political Parties*, will never be able to give "the tender and divining attention" required to understand the meaning of the cries of the oppressed (LPW 106/EL 14). "The same thing is the case to a lesser degree," she continues, "for the organizations that imitate, by contamination, the parties, which is to say, when public life is dominated by the competition of the parties; all organizations are included here, including, for example, the unions and even the churches" (LPW 106/EL 14). This is her critique of collectivity, as indicated in the title of her manuscript. It is a critique that applies to predominant practices of human rights as international law today. As Moyn recounts, "Human rights were forced to move not simply from morality to politics, but also from charisma to bureaucracy."[23] This shift in position hinders human rights actors from asking the afflicted Weil's central ethical question: *What are you going through?*

* * *

If the party spirit has contaminated all institutions, then what is needed is not reformation so much as transformation and, perhaps better but more difficult, invention. Weil writes, "Above the institutions that are meant to protect rights, persons, and democratic liberties, it is necessary to invent other ones [*il faut en inventer*] that are meant to discern and to abolish all that which, in contemporary life, buries the soul under injustice, lies, and ugliness" (LPW 128/EL 39). She elaborates on her word choice: "It is necessary to invent them [*Il faut les inventer*], for they are unknown [*inconnues*], and it is impossible to doubt that they are indispensable" (LPW 129/EL 39). I read this line, the concluding line of the essay, as arguing against both a return to a more classical political form (for instance, the argument that a better politics of the present is to be found in Ancient Greek texts) and a perfection of a current imperfect form (for instance, the Kantian and Hegelian claim that the ideal state can be realized and itself provides the means, such as rights to speech and assembly, to do so). Invention implies neither return nor reform.

It is worth noting here that Weil elaborated on her critique of human rights in "Human Personality" in her final magnum opus, *The Need for Roots*. She begins that text as follows: "The notion of obligations comes before that of rights, which is subordinate and relative to the former" (NR 3/6). This subordination is due to the fact, Weil thinks, that whereas an unrecognized obligation "loses none of its full force of existence," an unrecognized right "is not worth very much" (NR 3/6). Here she offers an ontology of obligations that will sound to scholars of rights like a revival of a natural rights tradition, only through the language of obligations and not rights.

Weil specifies her distinction between obligations and rights. "The actual relationship between the two," she says, "is as between object and subject" (NR 3/6). When one pauses to reflect on one's own social role, one has duties; when one looks at others, they have rights. And to them one has rights. And so on. Again, here she returns to a pre-political sense of obligation: "A man left alone in the universe would have no rights whatever, but he would have obligations" (NR 4/6). Moreover, we quickly come to see that for her in *The Need for Roots*, obligations belong not just to any pre-political realm, but to a theological one. Whereas "[r]ights are always found to be related to certain conditions," "[o]bligations alone remain independent of conditions" (NR 4/7). That is, "[t]hey belong to a realm situated above all conditions, because it is situated above this world" (NR 4/7). In a discussion beyond the scope of this book, we can note here that Weil's late political philosophy relies on the metaphysics she has been developing since her mystical contacts with Christ. But for now we can consider further her critique of rights at the outset of *The Need for Roots*.

In that final text, as in "Human Personality," she returns to the events of the French Revolution. Her initial concern with 1789 is that the revolutionaries "did not recognize the existence of such a realm," that is, of a supernatural realm (NR 4/7). "All they recognized was the one on the human plane" (NR 4/7). This secularism, to put it one way, immediately introduces a problem for Weil: they attempted to use the (particular) language of rights "to postulate absolute principles" (NR 4/7). This is a "confusion of language" because rights are contingent and conditional—rights imply an all-too-human attempt to realize justice. In its own idiosyncratic way, Weil's point here resonates with Marxists who, following Marx's critique of rights in "On the Jewish Question," have worried about how claims to rights ensnare actors in the operative relationships of force, especially conditions of private property. Her point also resonates to some extent with contemporary abolitionists who worry that rights language advances a reformist imaginary that has proven insufficient in the wake of ongoing racialized violence in our time.

Weil goes on to consider how obligations and rights set up different relationships between the individual and the collectivity. "Obligations are only binding on human beings," she writes (NR 4/7). "There are no obligations for collectivities, as such" (NR 4/7). "But," she says, "they exist for all human beings who constitute, serve, command or represent a collectivity, in that part of their existence which is related to the collectivity as in that part which is independent of it" (NR 4/7). The introductory section to *The Need for Roots* from which I have gathered the above quotations is titled "The Needs of the Soul." For Weil, a collectivity has no soul. Nor can it think. Lacking a soul and a mind, a collectivity also lacks obligations. Weil's initial point here, as she raises the topic of a new politics in France by revisiting one of the most important years in French history through her mystical lens, is to stress the need for French citizens to rebuild France with a view toward fulfilling each person's obligations, and thus to correct the limits of the 1789 Revolution.

As I read the first few pages of *The Need for Roots*, a text I will return to in the next and final chapter, I see Weil acknowledging the importance of rights more charitably than she does in "Human Personality." Her acknowledgement starts from a place not of a changed position—she remains decidedly critical of rights—but from a place of stressing that it matters greatly on what the post-occupation French collectivity founds itself. She is saying, from the very beginning of *The Need for Roots*, that France should not repeat its mistake of 1789, namely, founding itself on rights instead of on obligations. Rights are the object of her critique; obligation is the concept she promotes. It is that simple—the clarity of a dying philosopher's pen, not unlike the sharp distinctions Frantz Fanon makes in his final book, *The Wretched of the Earth*.

In her critique of rights in *The Need for Roots*, Weil once again has Maritain in mind. She quotes his line that rights are deeper than obligations because God has a right over creatures, and then comments, "Neither the notion of obligation nor that of right is compatible with God, but infinitely less so that of right" (NR 274–75/181). Rights are further from God, as it were, because any right "is mixed up with good and evil . . . the possession of a right implies the possibility of making either a good or a bad use of it," whereas, again, "the performance of an obligation is always, unconditionally, a good from every point of view" (NR 275/182). Rights are possessed and can be used to promote or limit justice. Obligations are performed; put differently, Weil here stresses that *activity* constitutes obligations.

For Weil, to say that God holds a sovereign right promotes a theology of power. Because "[a] sovereign right is the right of property according to the Roman idea," "[t]o ascribe to God sovereign rights without obligations is to turn him into the infinite equivalent of a Roman slave-holder" (NR 275/182). Weil's concern is not just theological but also with what such a theology implies in human affairs. To make God a holder of rights—to inject the supernatural with a modern political concept—"can only allow for a servile devotion" (NR 275/182). In other words, not only does Weil think Maritain's political theory is misguided, but she also thinks that his theology is anesthetic. A worshipper with a rights-holding God in mind cannot be more than a servant looking upon his master. By contrast, Weil wants to maintain "[t]he love which drives a free man to bring himself body and soul into servitude to whatever constitutes perfect good"—in other words, she wants to maintain "the opposite of a servile love [*le contraire d'un amour servile*]" (NR 275/182). Her critique of sovereign rights on the theological level resonates with her critique of property rights among humans.

Before drawing some lessons from late Weil's critique of rights, I want to stress one element of Weil's readings of rights in *The Need for Roots*. After clearly advancing obligations as a concept over rights, she goes on to say that recognizing such obligations—and she means the unconditional and pre-political obligation each human has toward every other human "for the sole reason that he or she is a human being"—"is expressed in a confused and imperfect form, that is, more or less imperfect according to the particular case, by what are called positive rights" (NR 5/7, 6/8). "To the extent to which positive rights are in contradiction with it," she goes on, "to that precise extent is their origin an illegitimate one" (NR 5/8). What is noteworthy here is that Weil underscores *positive* rights, qualifying their goodness by tying it to realizing obligations. The rights foregrounded in the 1789 "Declaration of the Rights of Man and Citizen" are "liberty, property, security, and resistance to oppression." Liberty, property, and resistance to oppression all arguably fit into the category of negative rights more easily than into that of positive rights.

What I am suggesting very briefly here, then, is that part of Weil's corrective to rights discourse is to call for the need of positive rights (in alignment with her sense of obligation) in creating a new community. *Pace* Edward Andrew, while I agree that in general Weil "understands rights [both] to be the expression of noisy clamor rather than mute oppression" and "to be, essentially, negotiable demands of commercial contractualism rather than inalienable and common possessions," I think it is too quick to say she considers rights "to be option-rights rather than welfare-rights."[24] Indeed, it is easy to read Weil's critique of using positive rights to achieve obligations for what she says, namely, that positive rights are confused and imperfect. It is more difficult to see this line for what she doesn't say directly there, namely, that all social forms are confused and imperfect, and that positive rights (not negative rights) can be a (limited) part of realizing obligations.

My reading is one way to track how Weil's Marxism continued through her mystical experiences. Like any socialist, she calls for a better alignment of positive rights with their theoretical intentions, and she leaves negative rights relatively unmentioned and ultimately criticized by way of implication with the (misoriented) focus of 1789. Later in the text she will criticize how property rights are used to dispossess peasants of their land: "Nothing can justify the property rights of a townsman over a piece of land [*Rien ne peut légitimer un droit de propriété d'un citadin sur une terre*]" (NR 82/61). She goes a step further, calling for the land to be transferred to the peasants and envisioning work occurring there through "extensive methods of cultivation cooperatively over vast areas owned by them in common" (NR 83/61).

My point in reading briefly Weil's critique of rights in *The Need for Roots* is to show my reader how she approached the concept with a view toward rebuilding a collective. But Weil's position is not my own. I find her critique of rights to be a helpful reminder to any city or country looking to recreate itself: after all, too often political organizations such as the Carter Center try to "develop" other countries by offering them a model of rights-based Western governance (a "democracy" program). But note that Weil's critique of rights here is not the anti-colonial critique. It is, if anything, a theological critique. Writing in the wake of Hannah Arendt's critique of natural rights in *Origins of Totalitarianism*, I remain skeptical of any call for a pre-political concept, here obligations, that can reorient the polis toward just ends. To affirm with Weil "an obligation towards every human being for the sole reason that he or she is a human being" sounds to my ear too much like a wishful call simply to recognize human rights more fully (NR 5/7). Would that a sense of obligation—for Weil "an eternal one"—actually impel just action (NR 5/8). It seems to me that we have to do better in articulating an ethics in this world so thoroughly contaminated by force. But my own critique of Weil, perhaps understood as reading her earlier work against her later work, does not at all mean that I find no promise in her critique of rights.

APPLYING WEIL'S CRITIQUE OF RIGHTS

To think further with Weil about human rights, we might inquire into the final term she wrote on the title of her "Human Personality" manuscript, the term I have yet to discuss in detail in this essay: justice. I suggest that Weil's critique of Personalism and her critique of human rights gives justice-oriented actors three things today.

First, Weil's critique of Personalism pushes us to ask constantly the practical question of our ethical and political concepts: Can a concept prevent the powerful from harming the weak? Does "person" do the work it says it does? Does "human rights"? When these concepts are found to be insufficient, that is, when we have errors in our vocabulary, we should work to redescribe our foundational political concepts—or, when necessary, to invent new terms that provide an alternative normative context in which our institutions are situated. In turn, these terms should be subject to intensive practical questioning. As philosopher Eduardo Mendieta has noted in an interview on politicizing rights, it is not just this latter, critical role, but also the former, inventive role that is the task of political philosophy: "[P]hilosophy is about generating new terms, new ways of thinking and saying what we are just beginning to realise."[25]

Second, discussions of human rights are too often academic and bureaucratic exercises, disconnected from everyday life by a human rights imaginary that includes the extremes of the halls of power and the camps of the powerless. When I talk to my students or rights advocates who work in NGOs about human rights, it is easy to get the impression that the work of human rights includes New York and Geneva, on the one hand, and the refugee camps of Greece, Kenya, and Sudan, on the other. Lest we cede practices that respond to human rights violations to only lawyers, aid workers, professors, and volunteers, we would do well to note how Weil commits herself to her critique of rights in a more quotidian, and thus more generally accessible, way.

Before fleeing Vichy France, Weil attended the court trials of immigrants—forced laborers—from French Indochina. Her friends noted that she attended these trials not out of curiosity but out of compassion.[26] Weil's method late in her life echoes her early practical insight: she continued not only to inquire into matters of her time but also to test her ideas in actions. She not only wrote on behalf of migrant workers the French state forced to work in Marseilles, but she also stood with them at their court trials and in their community meetings. This sense of a practical political philosophy is noteworthy. It provides a check against the tendency of we theorists of human rights, humanitarianism, globalization, and migration to distance ourselves too much from the lived circumstances of those we claim to defend. Too much of a distance results in a position of pity, not charity—of pseudo-generous philanthropy and not solidarity.

A third offering from Weil asks that we examine thoroughly the language of the "human." Although Weil—following Plato's critique of the Great Beast—was skeptical of collectivity in a context where the party spirit had infected all social spheres, she was also interested in forming new institutions. Regarding this constructive task, we might ask to what extent rights claims are helpful in bringing about these new institutions, including critiquing and making demands on present institutions with a view toward opening space for alternative performances and sites.

One concern is that rights claims individualize; they are part of the harmonization of the individual and the state. As literary theorist Joseph Slaughter notes about human rights as international law, human rights function "to normalize, publicize, and disseminate both its plot of human personality development and responsibility for it, so that rebellion—as an act of collective self-assertion—might be trans-plotted into socially acceptable modes of narrative protest that make individual claims on the state."[27] There is a narrative, Slaughter is pointing out, to human rights: just as it is the individual whose story is told in the narrative of becoming a subject, so too is it the individual who makes claims on the state.

If human rights are the language of minimal public demands, having displaced the maximal demands of decolonial movements by arguing for reformation instead of acting for transformation, then the individual (instead of the community or collective) is the category through which they minimize demands. "Human rights are typically concerned with cruelty to individuals," anthropologist Talal Asad observed in his famous critique about what human rights do and what they miss, and a focus on cruelty done to an individual misses structural forces and harms to collectives, such as cultural groups.[28] As Whyte puts it in a helpful phrase commenting on Asad's essay, the discourse of human rights both implies and produces "a prescriptive form of human subjectivity."[29] A Weil-inspired critique of human rights today might very well begin from the category of the human, noting how it serves to individualize politics and shift the scene of the political from public spaces of collective action to the theater that is the courtroom. Ayça Çubukçu has begun such a critique of the human.

Çubukçu observes that to widen the scope of the human in human rights assumes as a good an inclusion in "the family of humanity" (to use the language of the Universal Declaration). "But this tradition of thinking," she continues, "ignores the fact that the ideal of humanity and its conceptual and practical history have always involved the withdrawal of solidarity and the denial of equality to certain human beings whose humanity, as membership in a species, has nevertheless been granted."[30] Hence her claim about what her title, "Thinking Against Humanity," implies:

> Thinking against humanity is not thinking against solidarity or equality, nor is it refusing to act for a justice without borders. Thinking against humanity affirms the need for creating a common ground, and horizon, of political action in terms of what we want, and do not want, to see happen on this earth, whoever this "we" may be, when certainly, we are not unified as one humanity.[31]

To my ear, this is an invitation to practice a solidarity that is strong not in its unity but precisely in its recognition of opacity, to borrow the poet and philosopher Édouard Glissant's term.[32] Çubukçu sketches initial steps: "[W]e could practise principles of equality and solidarity across species without claiming membership in that part of humanity, proper humanity, which becomes proper at the expense of others who remain not properly human."[33] This is a way of co-constituting interspecies justice as we build communities worth defending.

To think against the centrality of the human in our time, as Weil rejected the person in hers, is to begin a pursuit of justice that is constructive—perhaps even reparative or corrective. To avoid inclusion does not prevent, but might in fact radically enable, a more effective stance of standing-with those afflicted by human rights violations. To think with Weil in the present pushes us not only to nuanced critiques of force, political minimalism, and a philanthropy that is a shadow of solidarity but also to a more quotidian sense of justice from which we build alternative futures.

As powerful as I find Çubukçu's suggestion, and as much as I agree with where her conclusion points us (a common solidarity based on a new vocabulary), I worry that abandoning the organizing frame of "the human" and "human rights" departs too quickly from a contaminated concept, certainly, but also a concept with immense legibility and therefore one that can remain a starting point for pursuing wider solidarities. To conclude this chapter, then, I suggest that we can read Weil against Weil: we can read her stress on solidarity as a reason to maintain the language of human rights. For what Weil's critique misses, in its thoroughgoing condemnation of rights, is what Hannah Arendt refuses to relinquish, namely, the perplexities of human rights. Arendt is clear that stateless people demonstrate the limits of understanding human rights as natural rights. "The world found nothing sacred in the abstract nakedness of being human," she wrote famously in *Origins of Totalitarianism*.[34] But she did not abandon rights discourse due to its contaminations by the market or due to its tie to a misguided idea of natural rights.

In her recent book *Rightlessness in an Age of Rights*, political theorist Ayten Gündoğdu combines what we might call Arendt's appreciation for the paradoxes of rights with Weil's demand to consider how rights play out in everyday life. Much like Weil in Marseilles, Gündoğdu attends to "the fragility of the guarantees that international human rights law offers for the legal personhood of migrants."[35] Gündoğdu's move—which I think is helpful for those of us who want to follow Weil—injects Arendtian thinking: "The Arendtian framework that I propose . . . refuses to see these perplexities [of rights] as dead ends . . . instead, it takes them as challenging political and ethical dilemmas that can be navigated differently, including the ways that bring to view new understandings of the relationships between rights, citizenship, and humanity."[36] Ultimately, I suggest, if we want to follow Weil's critique of human rights, then we need to maintain an opening for how rights claims can be deployed strategically even in our all-too-creaturely, decidedly imperfect, neoliberal moment.

NOTES

1. See Elizabeth Borgwardt, *A New Deal for the World: America's Vision for Human Rights* (Cambridge, MA: Harvard University Press, 2007).

2. Whyte, *The Morals of the Market*, 3.

3. Jayan Nayar, "The Non-Perplexity of Human Rights," *Theory & Event*, 22, no. 2 (2019): 278.

4. Samuel Moyn, *Human Rights and the Abuses of History* (New York: Verso, 2011), 2.

5. Ibid.

6. Ayça Çubukçu, "Thinking Against Humanity," *London Review of International Law* 5, no. 2 (2017): 252.

7. Ibid., 265–66.

8. Kinsella, "Of Colonialism and Corpses," 90.

9. To reiterate: "prestige" is a technical term in her work. As she wrote in 1936, "One must choose between prestige and peace. And whether one claims to believe in the fatherland, democracy, or revolution, the policy of prestige means war [*Il faut choisir entre le prestige et la paix. Et qu'on se réclame de la patrie, de la démocratie ou de la révolution, la politique de prestige, c'est la guerre*]" (FW 258/EHP II, 29).

10. Edward Andrew, "Simone Weil on the Injustice of Rights-Based Doctrines," *Review of Politics* 48, no. 1 (1986): 65.

11. Ibid., 66.

12. Ibid., 70.

13. Ibid., 67.

14. See Joseph R. Slaughter, *Human Rights Inc.: The World Novel, Narrative Form, and International Law* (New York: Fordham University Press, 2007). See also Angela Naimou, *Salvage Work: U.S. and Caribbean Literatures amid the Debris of Legal Personhood* (New York: Fordham University Press, 2015).

15. Andrew summarizes: "A human being, for Weil, is more than the sum total of the particular roles he adopts, or the *personae* he assumes. One's humanity is that which underlies the Hobbesian role, outward appearance, or mask which constitutes one's legal, social or moral *persona*. That which is the whole or holy is more than the sum of the parts one plays. Respect for persons is reverence for a role which is not usually understood to be a role . . . Weil's emphasis on the impersonal stresses what is common to all humans rather than what is unique, different, distinctive, or distinguished" (Andrew, "Simone Weil," 62, 63).

16. See Jacques Maritain, *Natural Law and Human Rights*. Quoted in Samuel Moyn, "Personalism, Community, and the Origin of Human Rights," in *Human Rights in the Twentieth Century*, ed. Stefan-Ludwig Hoffman (New York: Cambridge University Press, 2011), 94.

17. Moyn, "Personalism," 86.

18. See Perrin v. United States, 444 U.S. 37 (1979).

19. Samuel Moyn, *The Last Utopia: Human Rights in History* (Cambridge, MA: Belknap Press of Harvard University, 2010), 171.

20. Whyte, *Morals*, 93.

21. Ibid., 32–33.

22. I have inquired into the relevance of rights claims for organizing movements and not (simply) holding the state accountable. See Benjamin P. Davis, "The Promises of Standing Rock: Three Approaches to Human Rights," *Humanity: An International Journal of Human Rights, Humanitarianism, and Development* 12, no. 2 (2021): 205–25.

23. Moyn, *The Last Utopia*, 219.

24. Andrew, "Simone Weil," 75.

25. Kojo Koram and Enrique Prieto-Rios, "Decolonising Epistemologies, Politicising Rights: An Interview with Eduardo Mendieta," *Birkbeck Law Review* 3, no. 1 (2015): 19.

26. Perrin and Thibon, *Simone Weil as We Knew Her*, 31.

27. Slaughter, *Human Rights*, 91.

28. See Talal Asad, "What Do Human Rights Do? An Anthropological Enquiry," *Theory & Event* 4, no. 4 (2000).

29. Jessica Whyte, "Human Rights and the Collateral Damage of Neoliberalism," *Theory & Event* 20, no. 1 (2017): 139.

30. Çubukçu, "Thinking," 253.

31. Ibid., 266.

32. For my treatment of Glissant's concept, see Benjamin P. Davis, "The Politics of Édouard Glissant's Right to Opacity," *The CLR James Journal: The Journal of the Caribbean Philosophical Association* 25, nos. 1–2 (2019): 59–70.

33. Çubukçu, "Thinking," 266.

34. Hannah Arendt, *The Origins of Totalitarianism* (Boston: Mariner, 2001), 299.

35. Ayten Gündoğdu, *Rightlessness in an Age of Rights: Hannah Arendt and the Contemporary Struggles of Migrants* (New York: Oxford University Press, 2015), 18.

36. Ibid., 5.

Chapter 5

Construction of Belonging in an Uprooted World

On Tuesday, April 20, 2021, a Hennepin County jury declared the former Minneapolis police officer Derek Chauvin guilty on all three counts: manslaughter, third-degree murder, and second-degree murder. I was then living in the Cities, what those of us from Minnesota call Minneapolis and St. Paul, and I remember driving with my brother and his partner to see Minneapolis in light of the verdict. Starting from my brother's apartment by the Raymond Avenue light rail stop, we passed Workhorse, the café we frequented then, outside of which two National Guard Humvees and a City of St. Paul police car remained stationed, as they had been for the final days of the trial. We drove downtown and saw, surrounding the skyscrapers home to some of Minnesota's most valuable corporations, chain-link fence emerging from the cement barricades and topped with razor wire just so we got the message—"it feels strange, like I'm in a movie or something," Minneapolis's newspaper of record, the *Star Tribune*, quoted a seventeen-year-old saying the day before the verdict.[1] The ground level of all the shops near the Hennepin County Courthouse was boarded up, and while graffiti dotted some of the sheets of plywood, others were premade into advertisements reading "Retail Open." In other words, we drove amidst a dystopian landscape where the military patrolled—but where you could still shop. Weil's words echoed in my mind: "Where force is absolutely sovereign, justice is absolutely unreal" (NR 240/160). In her terms, the scene downtown was uprooted: where people misoriented themselves to the abstractions of money and status (through what they drive, wear, and eat), and where state force reigned, rendering justice impossible—despite the verdict—until the community cultivated a more just city.

From downtown we headed south to participate in the mourning and celebration at George Floyd Square. We somehow found a parking spot on Chicago Avenue and walked amongst strangers to the Cup Foods. Eventually heading back to the car, we stopped at the Nokomis Gallery at the Chicago Avenue Fine Arts Center. Most of the gallery's collection related to the 2020–2021 uprisings. One of the preserved signs read

> What if 2020 isn't cancelled? What if 2020 is the year we've been waiting for? A year so uncomfortable, so painful, so scary, so raw—that it finally forces us to grow. A year that screams so loud, finally awakening us from our ignorant slumber . . . A year we finally band together, instead of pushing each other further apart.

The gallery was getting crowded, and the person in charge said loudly, "Capacity, capacity. This is what community looks like, people. We gotta let people know we are at capacity." This was a moment of anarchy, meaning people were going about their complicated relations without the mediation of repressive state forces. I left the gallery. An activist outside of Cup Foods was calling out progressive pastors for not sending a strong enough message to their congregations—for hiding behind the language of "peace" in a context where police and military units still controlled much of the city, meaning what we were there to mourn together could happen again at any time. Weil would refer to such a structure as the force that kills not yet (cf. SWA 184–85).

We walked from the Nokomis Gallery to pay our respects at Say Their Names Cemetery, which included plastic grave markers to honor George Floyd, Breonna Taylor, Philando Castile, Emmett Till, and others. "Rest in Power" is written across each headstone. Anna Barber and Connor Wright, two artists quarantining in 2020 in Chicago and Philadelphia, respectively, came up with the idea for the cemetery as they stared down a news feed with a growing list of Black names killed by police. The point, Barber said, is "to allow people to visualize and humanize these lists."[2] Chicago Avenue felt more open and significantly less forceful than 6th Street downtown. No police were in sight. The Avenue was, as it had been for about a year, something of an experiment. With Weil, we could describe the scene along Chicago Avenue as root-fixing: people questioned the vocabulary of the day ("peace"), celebrated those who died too soon, and attempted to live in a way that did not rely on oppressive and repressive state force.

As the verdict for the case neared, the state's occupation of the Cities expanded beyond its usual focus, such that the Cities in their entirety felt occupied. In a February 28, 2021, op-ed titled "Minneapolis Doesn't Need a National Guard Occupation" and published in the *Star Tribune*, Sheila Nezhad addressed Minneapolis Mayor Jacob Frey's request that Governor Tim Walz mobilize the National Guard for the trial of the police officer who murdered George Floyd. Herself in the running for mayor, she asked Mayor

Frey to reconsider his request for mobilization.[3] She noted that "[t]he residents of Minneapolis have the right to petition their government and otherwise exercise their constitutional rights to speech and assembly." Importantly, she argued that in some way the city already felt occupied, and that adding the Guard would be an intensification, not a different form of governance: "Occupation by the Guard will only add to the militarism by the Minneapolis police, Hennepin County Sheriff's Department and Minnesota State Patrol." And she observed further: "The tank-like vehicles, troop carriers, Humvees and SUVs rode up and down our streets supposedly to discourage agitators, but rather instilled fear in community members."

She then corrected the official story: it was not the Guard but community members, in the form of mutual-aid groups, who "set up tents and tables to provide food and water, and to distribute flashlights and generators when power was cut to 'riot' areas." "Neighbors met each other, some for the first time, to organize block patrols and make sure everyone had someone to call when they needed help." As a result of this mutual aid, she wrote, "Our grief was met with humanity, not helicopters and Humvees."

Nezhad's op-ed offered a narrative different from that of the state. Her article preceded a March 7, 2021, op-ed written by Major General Shawn Manke of the Minnesota National Guard, which was also published in the *Star Tribune* and titled "Minnesota National Guard is Here to Protect People, Their Rights and Their Property."[4] There Manke argued that "[o]ur members provided security and helped re-establish peace and stability to a chaotic environment." Like the activist outside Cup Foods on April 20, Nezhad had already correctly questioned any claim that there was "peace" in Minnesota communities before George Floyd's murder. The major general further claimed that the role of the Guard is to "support communities, law enforcement agencies, and other interagency partners in ensuring peace, protecting people and property, and enabling the peaceful exercise [of] their First Amendment rights." Nezhad had also anticipated this line, noting that the presence of the Guard in fact prevents citizens both from feeling that they can peacefully protest and from actually doing so (by assaulting protestors, for instance).

Nezhad's op-ed not only challenged the predictable lines of the military leader writing on behalf of the state and of property holders. It also provides a point of contrast with sophisticated theory that avoids making claims to rights or using generalizations such as "humanity." I raise this point here, following my argument to keep the language of rights and humanity in the previous chapter, to highlight some of the language used on the ground in occupied Minneapolis.

The combined police and military occupation in Minneapolis recalled for many refugees living in the Cities the war-torn contexts from which they fled. "I came to the United States thinking this is going to be a peaceful place where I could heal from all those trauma," Zaynab Abdi, who fled Somalia for Yemen before going to Egypt and then Minnesota, told a reporter a few days after the verdict.[5] "[Y]et those trauma are coming back and becoming more worse," she continued. "Seeing all this military presence is increasing this fear." "This feels like the beginning of war," Abdishakur Elmi, who migrated from Somalia to North America in the 1990s added. "It has really affected our mental health."

* * *

Occupation is nothing new in the United States. Indigenous lands remain occupied by U.S. settlers with police backing. In *The Counterrevolution: How Our Government Went to War Against Its Own Citizens*, lawyer and political scientist Bernard Harcourt explains that "[t]he central tenet of counterinsurgency theory is that populations—originally colonial populations, but now *all* populations, including our own—are made up of a small active minority of insurgents, a small group of those opposed to the insurgency, and a large passive majority that can be swayed either way."[6] The task of counterinsurgency is to influence the majority—meaning that "counterinsurgency is not just a military strategy, but more importantly a political technique."[7] Counterinsurgency is now deployed more widely "at home"—beyond, and following from, military and police force in other countries, on Indigenous land, and in neighborhoods where predominantly people of color live. When the police quell protests in Ferguson, at Standing Rock, or in Minneapolis, they are attempting to win the hearts and minds of U.S. citizens. Hence the Major General's op-ed.

In light of the above testimonies and this broader context, in April 2021 I started to reread *The Need for Roots* through the lens of what a community could look like in the wake of occupation.[8] Speaking to our present of occupation and domestic counterinsurgency, this final chapter focuses on not yet another of Weil's critiques but instead on what Weil wanted, in the last years of her life, to construct: a more just—and more beautiful—political community in the wake of German-occupied France. In other words, Weil's relationship to collectivity changed to some extent. Tasked to outline a plan for France's renewal, she shifted how she leveraged her longstanding Platonic critique of the Great Beast in order to consider the question of creating a collectivity that could approximate a just social balance. And so she starts *The Need for Roots* not with a dismissal of the passions that drive collective life but with a recognition of the importance of that life: "[W]e owe our respect to a collectivity, of whatever kind—country, family or any other—not for itself, but because it is food for a certain number of human souls" (NR 8/9).

But before I read *The Need for Roots* as a text offering public paths for community organizing in the wake of occupation, I need to contextualize Weil's discussion.

THE NEED FOR ROOTS IN CONTEXT

In mid-1942 Weil was living in New York, to which she had fled from Marseilles. She passed through Morocco on her way to the United States, embarking on June 7 on the Portuguese ship *Serpa Pinto*, which stopped in Bermuda and disembarked in New York on July 7. After briefly staying in a hotel, the Weil family moved into an apartment at 549 Riverside Drive. Away from the suffering of France, Weil felt deserted in New York. She wrote to influential French philosopher Jacques Maritain and to U.S. and British military officers with a view toward implementing her plan of frontline nurses.[9] When she heard that police killed two women at a patriotic demonstration in Marseilles on July 14, she did not eat for two days.[10] By mid-summer she was depressed. Moreover, her headaches returned, and she often spent whole days on the floor in her sleeping bag.[11] Feeling too far removed from suffering, she considered moving to the south to work alongside agricultural laborers. With Simone Deitz, another French woman, whom Weil knew in Marseilles and met in the waiting room at the French consulate, Weil enrolled in a first-aid course in Harlem; all of the other students were Black.[12] She also spent time in New York's public libraries in order to "dig into the hidden recesses of theology."[13]

Weil's continuing efforts to work with the most oppressed and precarious members of a society—women factory workers around Paris, migrants forced to work in Marseilles, and now Black workers in New York—offer more than a masochistic drive for martyrdom or some false identification with the worse off. Rather, her efforts reflect her belief that academic theory is not sufficient for comprehending how social relations function. Her efforts also underscore her understanding that a society actually attentive to its most exploited, abjected, and oppressed would be a remade society. As a leading voice in Black Studies, Rinaldo Walcott, writes, "Black freedom is not just freedom for Black subjects; it is a freedom that inaugurates an entirely new human experience for everyone."[14] "This is not an exceptionalist argument on behalf of Black people," he goes on, "but an accounting of the ways that Black people's dispossession and its possible rectification would require global reordering, rethinking, and remaking; such an accounting would mean a reorientation of the planet and all modes of being human on it."[15] Weil understood that rectifying dispossession implied a global reordering of social life. One way of reading how she placed herself throughout her life is to see it as part of her method to understand the world. She knew staying within her elite milieu would hinder her understanding of social life. Perhaps she started from the most dispossessed communities in order to learn about paths for the kind of rectification Walcott highlights.

By mid-September 1942, Weil's spirits had risen because she had hope that she would be able to sail to London. The well-connected Maurice Schumann had spoken about Weil to André Philip, a former socialist deputy who was sent to London by the Resistance and appointed de Gaulle's Commissioner for the Interior in July.[16] With this possibility on the horizon, Weil started to write more frequently, filling notebook after notebook from mid-September onward.[17] In October Philip arrived in the United States to lobby President Roosevelt to adopt a more favorable attitude toward the Free French movement. While in New York Philip interviewed Weil, and this interview resulted in the understanding that Weil would join his staff in London.[18] The Allied landing in north Africa occurred on November 8. On November 10, 1942, after saying goodbye to her parents on the docks, Weil set sail to London on the Swedish freighter *Vaalaren*.

The cargo ship took about fifteen days to reach Liverpool from New York. There were ten passengers on the ship, and Weil took an active role in entertaining them through telling stories each night, including in the moonlight on the deck of the ship, notwithstanding the increased risk of being torpedoed. Still, she remained obsessed with returning to France, and on the ship she refused to eat more than the rations her compatriots were allowed during wartime. Likely because of her previous pacifist and Communist activities, in England she was held in a clearing center for eighteen days, until Maurice Schumann again intervened, this time by obtaining her release.[19] She was given a small office at 19 Hill Street in London. From this room she would write day and night for the next four months, sleeping around three hours each night. Her output in this period totaled nearly 800 printed pages.[20] Her essays included "Human Personality," "Draft for a Statement of Human Obligations," and "Is There a Marxist Doctrine?" Her writing, then, remained in the form of *pièces d'occasion*; she responded to the context into which she was thrown.

Weil lived for months at the French volunteers' barracks until finally finding a room in mid-January 1943 at 31 Portland Road, Holland Park—in a poor section of London, Notting Hill. There she lived with the widow of a schoolteacher.[21] Weil attended Mass almost every day at a Jesuit Church on Farm Street.[22] Despite liking London, she remained unhappy. She was not able to realize her plan of frontline nurses, and her attempt to enter France on a sabotage mission also did not come to fruition. That is, rather than serving the Resistance as she desired, she was—in a cruel irony given her early critique of bureaucracy—becoming a kind of civil servant. (Her criticism, it is worth noting, does not necessarily devalue those who dedicate their lives to civil service; it is more a criticism of how bureaucracies necessarily function.) By January 1943 Weil was filled with regret and remorse for having left France, and her headaches began again. Finally, having not been sent to France, and not wanting to be associated with the Free French movement when France was liberated, Weil resigned from the Free French in late July.[23]

Thus, living in poverty and exile, and commissioned by the Free French to write a report on the renewal of Europe, Weil wrote *The Need for Roots* in London from around November 1942 to sometime in the spring of 1943. Living in a country whose language and customs were not her own, and conflicted about her role in the renewal of the country she considered her own, she was especially concerned with how her native France would take shape when it was no longer occupied by foreign soldiers. Persecuted for her Jewish heritage, and writing from England, she was not theorizing about collectivity from a position of security or with the comforts of state protection. Rather, from a point of immediate precarity, she was trying to articulate a way for a people to move forward following immense destruction and military occupation.

Weil's positioning, what with decolonial thinker Walter Mignolo we could call her "locus of enunciation," matters for several reasons as we think about her shifting critique and construction of collectivity.[24] Weil wrote from a position of having almost nothing, save some of her books, her experiences, and her relationships. In other words, suffering persecution not for what she did but for who she was, Weil sketched a new, duty-bound collective not in order to keep her position, but in order to be able to have a position—that is, in order to envision a community in which she and others could live as who they are. By emphasizing duties, she sought to raise questions about what we owe one another as human beings—not just following immense violence, but what we've always owed one another simply by virtue of being human.

To consider Weil's importance to thinking in post-occupation contexts today, I will read part III of *The Need for Roots*, "The Growing of Roots." Because she is writing with a view toward constructing a political community and not simply critiquing an existing one, she relies on some terms—theoretical building blocks—to orient her readers. These terms include "prestige" and "civilization," two terms she had to a considerable extent been critical of previously. Some critical theorists today might find Weil's return to these terms unsettling—or worse, indicative of the fact that she lost her critical edge after her mystical experiences. Sensitive to these criticisms, I nevertheless maintain that, overall, Weil's stunning final book deserves close examination as we think through questions of belonging in the present, because her ability to combine spiritual depth and social justice speaks so incisively to our counterrevolutionary moment, in which many of us nevertheless aim to orient ourselves toward justice and to remake the contexts in which we find ourselves such that force no longer reigns as sovereign.

ROOTS

In offering my reading of Weil's concept of roots below, I will follow political theorist Antonio Vázquez-Arroyo's argument that in *The Need for Roots* "Weil casts political responsibility as a need of the soul."[25] I will also have in mind, and write informed by, contemporary painter José Parlá's exhibition *Roots*, which suggests that roots not only are tied to the past that informs the present but also can be expressed playfully and colorfully in creative engagements with the cities in which we live.

Weil begins her section "Uprootedness" in *The Need for Roots* with an explanation of the importance of roots:

> To be rooted is perhaps the most important and least recognized need of the human soul. It is one of the hardest to define. A human being has roots by virtue of his real, active and natural participation in the life of a community which preserves in living shape certain particular treasures of the past and certain particular expectations for the future. This participation is a natural one, in the sense that it is automatically brought about by place, conditions of birth, profession and social surroundings. Every human being needs to have multiple roots. It is necessary for him to draw wellnigh the whole of his moral, intellectual and spiritual life by way of the environment of which he forms a natural part. (NR 43)

> L'enracinement est peut-être le besoin le plus important et le plus méconnu de l'âme humaine. C'est un des plus difficiles à définir. Un être humain a une racine par sa participation réelle, active et naturelle à l'existence d'une collectivité qui conserve vivants certains trésors du passé et certains pressentiments d'avenir. Participation naturelle, c'est-à-dire amenée automatiquement par le lieu, la naissance, la profession, l'entourage. Chaque être humain a besoin d'avoir de multiples racines. Il a besoin de recevoir la presque totalité de sa vie morale, intellectuelle, spirituelle, par l'intermédiaire des milieux dont il fait naturellement partie. (NR 36)

Roots are material and concrete. By "real" she refers to quotidian tasks of working physically with others, such as picking grapes together in a vineyard. In this way, roots are communal: they are cultivated in participation with others, implying that planting and growing roots requires a community in which this active sharing-with occurs. Weil's targets—what lacks reality—are the abstractions she saw in the transactions of capitalism, the jargon of intellectualism, and the hierarchies and calculations of bureaucracy. These spheres of abstraction, as literary theorist Christy Wampole comments reading Weil, represent a world "becoming ever more remote from itself, replacing the real with empty figures."[26] Further, roots tie us to time: they are both retrospective and prospective, both preservative and expectative. In a figurative sense, roots move both backward and forward in time, in memories and dreams. That is, to be rooted is to attend to particularities of the past and the future—to both historical "particular treasures" and expectations. When one is rooted, one looks in both directions, having both histories and hopes. Roots are also culturally specific. Finally, we should not overlook that Weil's term is not "root" but "roots" in the plural. She adds later: "We must also keep . . . some arrangement whereby human beings may once more be able to recover their roots. This doesn't mean they should be fenced in . . . Rooting in and the multiplying of contacts are complementary to one another" (NR 52/42). Indeed, as living, roots change when being woven and performed in encounters both familiar and unexpected. In sum, Weil gives us a sketch of roots in a specific sense: roots are material, active, communal, participatory, temporal, living, particular, and plural—"a certain terrestrial poetry" (WG 67/124).

* * *

To state Weil's claim that roots are a human need in a different register, we could say that any new political community relies on a new sense of political belonging. To whom and to what do we belong? Philosopher Shannon Hoff has recently stressed the importance of this question through her reading of "the political significance of belonging."[27] "What matters to human individuals is not simply their capacity for self-determination," Hoff writes, "but the fact that other phenomena can appear as meaningful and important to them, demanding acknowledgement."[28] Her list of phenomena that demand acknowledgement includes "intimate others, the things they are involved in studying and learning, their family networks, their involvements in group activities, their religious commitments, [and] their opportunities for creative expression."[29] "We are oriented," Hoff continues, "toward contexts that are oriented around us (such as families and, in a different way, nation-states), around particular ideas and interests (such as scholarly and artistic worlds)" and further "around specific activities (such as sports and crafts), around specific beliefs and commitments (such as religious and activist communities), and so on."[30] Belonging, then, is always plural and overlapping: we can belong to a café, a church, and an online chat just as much as we feel we belong to a coalition, a community, or a country.

We can consider an example I heard at Workhorse: when a graphic designer moves to a new city and says, shyly, to the barista at a café, "I am hoping to set down roots here." "Rootedness," Wampole writes in studying the metaphor, "is a primary organizing trope that accommodates the need to feel connected to something outside the self."[31] "Across cultures and through time," she continues, "the root surfaces again and again as a figure for filiation, cultural connectedness, regional or national allegiance, and symbiosis with the environment."[32] Roots are helpful in part because we use them to learn something about ourselves.[33] The designer sees roots as stabilizing through the sense of place and history they invoke. But roots need not mean just where we were born. When we were driving through Minneapolis, my brother's partner, who is from Chicago, told me that he started to feel more strongly that he belonged in Minneapolis after a night in 2020 when police officers used their batons to beat him and his friends when they broke curfew to stand in solidarity with protestors. A couple in a van, strangers to my friend and his friends, picked them up and drove them home. For him, such an acknowledgement from strangers served as meaning-making; it demanded acknowledgment, in Hoff's terms.

Third, setting down roots, in the sense that the designer meant it at the café, is often necessary for survival amidst the precarious conditions of capitalism, especially for those who are oppressed given their identities. Setting down "roots" thus might mean a Muslim's ability to find a welcoming place to worship in a predominantly Christian city or a gay person's finding a home and a family in what otherwise often feels like a homophobic place. The hope to find roots, most basically, expresses a desire to participate in meaningful collective life; to continue the example, many Muslims and queer people in the Cities, from their place of rootedness, have made tremendous contributions to the wider collective life of the Cities. Roots for Weil, as for many uprooted people, are not something that can be taken for granted and easily dismissed as unnecessary. They are essential to who she takes herself to be, and, when taken from her, form her central preoccupation. As the examples of the religious and queer persons illustrate, a focus on roots does not necessarily suggest secret ethno-nationalist or totalitarian desires. Instead, with Weil roots are *contrasted* to national pride, involving instead a kind of compassion that is universal, meaning that it is able to cross borders and encourage tenderness, she writes, "over all countries in misfortune, over all countries without exception" (NR 172/116).

The objection that roots are necessarily totalitarian often comes from theorists trained in Continental philosophy around the time Rosi Braidotti was citing Gilles Deleuze to write about nomadic subjects. As An Yountae has noted in arguing that Braidotti misreads Édouard Glissant, "Braidotti's affirmation of movement and her model of the all-transcending and locatable subject raise questions of accountability to the sociohistorical location of the subject."[34] In turn Yountae asks: "[S]hould not the call for accountability and mourning for the loss and suffering of others precede the joyful celebration of freedom and nomadic ontology? Should not the question of the other be at the center of ethics rather than a preoccupation with the self's endless becoming?"[35] As I read Weil, roots are part of accounting to others. They serve as a check on endless self-becoming, and in this way follow conceptually from acknowledging the importance of our complicated or in-tension interior lives.[36] Second, the claim to roots as oppressive is often suggested without specifying historical context, thus universalizing a political strategy and, by doing so, completely missing, for example, histories of Indigenous struggles across the Americas, which—at Standing Rock, for the Xukuru in Brazil, and for other nations—often work through strong roots, literally and figuratively, to place, land, histories, and community, including a sense of a people, *povo*, or *pueblo*.[37]

Ultimately, for Weil it is not rootedness that leads to a doubling-down on the self and one's identity in violent ways against others, but uprootedness, which perpetuates itself. Weil thinks growing roots are the only way to confront the forces of fascism. "Totalitarianism's idolatrous course," she writes, "can only be arrested by coming up against a genuinely spiritual way of life [*une vie spirituelle authentique*]" (NR 91/66). It matters greatly how we orient ourselves, how we direct our lives, what we choose to worship, and those we choose to serve. Our very polity results from these choices.

UPROOTING

If roots suggest belonging, then is being uprooted simply the inverse, namely, a feeling of isolation? Indeed, what does it mean to be uprooted, and what forces uproot individuals and collectivities? Weil's own words merit more thorough study:

> Uprootedness is by far the most dangerous malady to which human societies are exposed, for it is a self-propagating one. For people who are really uprooted there remain only two possible sorts of behavior: either to fall into a spiritual lethargy resembling death, like the majority of slaves in the days of the Roman Empire, or to hurl themselves into some form of activity necessarily designed to uproot, often by the most violent methods, those who are not yet uprooted, or only partly so. (NR 47)

> Le déracinement est de loin la plus dangereuse maladie des sociétés humaines, car il se multiplie lui-même. Des êtres vraiment déracinés n'ont guère que deux comportements possibles: ou ils tombent dans une inertie de l'âme presque équivalente à la mort, comme la plupart des esclaves au temps de l'Empire romain, ou ils se jettent dans une activité tendant toujours à déraciner, souvent

par les méthodes les plus violentes, ceux qui ne le sont pas encore ou ne le sont
qu'en partie. (NR 39)

Uprootedness is not just a misfortune or a setback, such as getting dealt a
bad hand of cards or needing to take a detour to go around a car accident on
your way to work. To be uprooted, Weil diagnoses, is the worst thing that can
happen to an individual or a society. She explains two results of this condition. The first is a "spiritual lethargy." While she cites enslaved people under
Roman rule as her example, we might also consider the three or four hours of
television and three hours on their phones U.S. citizens spend each day and
thus the thousands of advertisements we are exposed to each day.[38]

The second result of being uprooted for Weil is that those uprooted start to
take up practices of uprooting. One crystal clear example of this is ongoing
U.S. occupation of countries in the Middle East. In response to our lifestyles
that demand constant resource extraction, we invade other countries. In so
doing we debase words such as "democracy" and "freedom." In our lack
of understandings of other spiritual, ethical, and political traditions, such
as Islam, we arrogate to ourselves the doling out of justice in contexts we
do not understand. This form of uprootedness has spread so widely in U.S.
society that it is not only the war hawks hollering that our soldiers need to
"save" Muslim women but even well-intentioned groups such as Amnesty
International. Indeed, in 2012 Amnesty International put placards around
Chicago for the North Atlantic Treaty Organization summit to argue that the
United States should not pull out its troops from Afghanistan. "NATO: Keep
the progress going!" read the posters, which featured as a photograph two
Afghani women wearing burkas covering their bodies, an image designed to
pander to U.S. citizens' facile equation of certain forms of clothing in predominantly Muslim countries with misogynist oppression.[39] The clear goal
of the advertising campaign was to keep the United States in Afghanistan
on behalf of the "human rights" of the women there. Overall in the United
States, the lack of knowledge of the socially, ethically, and politically robust
and multifaceted tradition that is Islam extends to such an extent that it
stretches the history of epistemology to use the word "knowledge" in association with it.

A key part of being uprooted is to lack a sense of history. This makes sense
given how Weil defines roots in terms of memories and hopes—spiritual
treasures from the past and communal dreams for the future. We can consider
for example cultural theorist Stuart Hall's comment on an English lack of
consciousness around its own colonial history in his 1978 essay "Racism
and Reaction": "To hear problems of race discussed in England today, you
would sometimes believe that relations between British people and peoples
of the Caribbean or the Indian subcontinent began with the wave of black

immigrants in the late 1940s and 1950s," as opposed to beginning with British imperialism.[40] To put Hall's analysis in Weil's terms, we see here that it is the uprooted who perpetuate that condition. The English, without an understanding of their history, spiral into a form of popular authoritarianism that responds to an economic crisis with reactionary racism. "Race is the prism through which the British people are called upon to live through, then to understand, and then to deal with, the growing crisis," Hall writes.[41] The result includes "legal harassment of the black colony populations, the overt racist homilies against the whole black population by judges in courts, the imposition of tough policing and arrest on suspicion in the colony areas, the rising hysteria about black crime and the identification of black crime with 'mugging.'"[42]

In a polemical claim, Weil argues that France, as a colonial country, deserves its uprootedness at home. "If it were possible to reckon up exactly the factors which have contributed to our defeat [*notre désastre*]," she writes, "it would doubtless be found that all these things which have been our shame—like that one, and our colonial greediness, and our ill-treatment of foreigners—have each brought their individual and effective weight to bear in our general undoing" (NR 86/63). "A lot of things can be said about our misfortune," she concludes, "but not that it is undeserved" (NR 86/63). Leaving aside Weil's sense of a deserved punishment here, I want to stress her ability to see that a country's colonial projects contribute to its undoing—and that, moreover, a country's spiral into authoritarian populism results from applying its colonial methods to domestic "problems." Without suggesting that by any means she was the first person to make this point, I do want to make note of the fact that she wrote this claim here around 1943, seven years before it was circulated more widely through Aimé Césaire's 1950 *Discourse on Colonialism* and eight years before Hannah Arendt's 1951 *On the Origins of Totalitarianism*. The key point is that, as Inese Radzins comments, by the early 1940s Weil argued decisively that "it would be impossible for France to be rooted after the war, either socially or politically, if she participated in the destruction and uprooting of others."[43] "What Weil pointed to," Radzins continues, "was the dual nature of France's destruction—not only in oppressing others, but also by sanctioning this destruction through various policies at home."[44]

In sum, to start reading Weil's concept of uprootedness in terms of lacking history, and in particular through lacking knowledge of one's country's own (ongoing) colonial history, is to suggest that the growing of roots involves not simply a new-age feeling of being in touch with the world. Rather, for Weil, roots require a thoroughgoing *historical* understanding of where one comes from individually and collectively.

Weil explains several forces that generate uprootedness. Money and education, she says, are two poisons directly spreading the disease of uprootedness. She defines both terms expansively. By money she refers to an orientation to profit and capital gain at the expense of an ability to see the human relations on which both are based. By education she means a sense of French nationalism that spreads what she calls a false sense of greatness, which I will discuss further below. It is in part an orientation to money and false greatness (as opposed to a Platonic and Christian "Good") that Weil has in mind when she writes, "Uprooting breeds idolatry" (NR 68/52). Weil's critique of these forms of idolatry, Mary Dietz explains, offers a "therapeutic politics" that discloses "the mystique of *étatisme* that uproots political life, and the 'idolatry of self' that at once corrupts public morality and is also a sign of its corruption."[45] For Weil, military conquest also always generates uprootedness. Without exception, colonial methods produce uprootedness. To be rendered unemployed given the whims of the market is also to be uprooted. "It is urgent, therefore," Weil argues, "to consider a plan for reestablishing the working-class by the roots" (NR 73/55). In sum, a people is uprooted when they see the world through a capitalist lens, when they elevate their all-to-human collectivity to a status deserving worship, and when they lack daily work, which for late Weil is a kind of *metaxu* or mediation between the natural and the supernatural. An uprooted people uproots others in turn when they try to conquer or colonize them.

It is worthwhile to pause here to recall Weil's rhetorical strategy in commenting on uprootedness in *The Need for Roots*. In a method I think is worth following, what we might call writing against one's own nation-state, that is, critiquing it from within, Weil implicates her French readers in their own present condition of uprootedness. On Dietz's reading, Weil calls out the complicity of her readers because "they have warped the meaning of country by perpetuating a dangerous illusion that masquerades as country and a destructive spirit that parades as true patriotism"; "rather than fulfilling the need for roots," Dietz continues, "this national egoism perpetuates *déracinement*."[46] Weil's pointing out the complicity of her fellow French citizens proceeds through a critique of what they understand as a great civilization.

READING "THE GROWING OF ROOTS": A CRITIQUE OF CIVILIZATION

In keeping with the trajectory of this book, I will read *The Need for Roots* as offering a critique of "civilization"—or at least of a certain kind of civilization. While much scholarship on *The Need for Roots* focuses on how she opens the book by presenting a balance of "needs of the soul" and on how she closes the book with a call for work to be the "spiritual core" of a new civilization, my reading will focus on the earlier sections of part III, "The Growing of Roots." I will first treat the more surprising and problematic part of that section: Weil's endorsement of collectivity, including its prestige. I will then explain how she qualifies that endorsement through measured critiques of imperial civilization, of a false concept of greatness, of a sense of history that erases spiritual treasures, of a normative claim to progress, and of any justification of slavery. My concluding claim will be that Weil's key insight in *The Need for Roots*, read for the present, is her direction or reorientation of her reader to ongoing social and spiritual cultivation akin to an artistic process. Through Weil's take on the classical trope in political philosophy of politics as art, we gain the reminder that what we need to rebuild our communities is not to be found in an otherworldly realm but in some way is already here. Thus, one important political task is to listen to the ways that a "not yet" form of political life is already speaking.

Weil calls for a recovery of France's prestige [*grandeur*]. This is surprising because Weil had already worked out the connection between prestige and violence, particularly that of fascism, in her 1936 "Do We Have to Grease Our Combat Boots." There she writes, "One must choose between prestige and peace. And whether one claims to believe in the fatherland, democracy, or revolution, the policy of prestige means war" (FW 258/EHP II, 29). In *The Need for Roots*, despite her critique of the 1789 French revolutionaries' use of rights, she acknowledges that the revolution increased the country's international standing, such that other countries looked to it for direction regarding liberty and equality. Those countries cringed at the sight of an occupied France. Weil writes, "[T]he collapse of France was only deeply felt in places where the spirit of 1789 had left behind a legacy" (NR 195/130).

Weil also sees potential in France's difficult years. "The temporary laying low of France as a nation gives her the opportunity of becoming once again among nations what she was in the past, and what for a long time now people were hoping to see her become again—an inspiration" (NR 195/130). It is in this context that she appeals to prestige: "And for France to be able to recover her prestige in the world—a prestige which is indispensable to the very health of her inner life—she must become an inspiration before she has become again, thanks to the defeat of her enemies, a nation" (NR 195/130). Here the critical reader pauses, noticing how Weil's resuscitation of prestige is immediately tied to the nation.

Further, on the next page Weil calls for France, as part of recovering its prestige, to fulfill a "double mission": (a) "to help France to discover in the depths of her misfortune an inspiration in keeping with her genius and with the actual needs of mankind in distress"; and (b) "to spread this inspiration, once recovered or at any rate glimpsed, throughout the world" (NR 196/130).

While the first part of the double mission makes sense, the second is deeply troubling. How could Weil, one of the first European philosophers to understand that totalitarianism in Europe was a product of European colonial rule, return in her late writings to promote French expansion and imposition?

In addition to advancing a recovery of prestige, she calls for an orientation to a certain kind of civilization. "An educational method which is not inspired by the conception of a certain form of human perfection is not worth very much," she writes (NR 216/145). "When it is a matter of educating a whole people, this conception should be that of civilization" (NR 216/145). Here the reader once again pauses. As Martinican poet and philosopher Édouard Glissant argues, directly writing back to colonial France, "Through the entirely Western notion of civilization the experience of a society is summed up, in order to project it immediately into an evolution, most often an expansion as well."[47] We have already seen how Weil's appeal to prestige implies a will to expansion. "When one says civilization," Glissant concludes, "the immediate implication is a will to civilize. This idea is linked to the passion to impose civilization on the Other."[48] Weil, to her credit, seems aware of the European "will to civilize." The civilization she will call for is one that neither resembles a past civilization nor is found in a dream of a utopian one but rather is an inspiring civilization found, a bit mysteriously, "among the truths eternally inscribed in the nature of things" (NR 216/145). It is through her critique of civilization that in the section "The Growing of Roots" Weil regains her critical impulse, in particular through her critiques not just of civilization but also of history, progress, slavery, and the colonization of Columbus. In order to show the kind of society Weil warns against in offering her post-occupation plan for construction, I will treat these critiques in turn.

Weil claims there are four obstacles to reaching a spiritually sound, properly oriented civilization: "[O]ur false conception of greatness; the degradation of the sentiment of justice; our idolization of money; and our lack of religious inspiration" (NR 216/145). She writes in the first-person plural "without any hesitation," because she doubts that "at the present moment there is a single human being on the surface of the globe who is free from that quadruple defect and more doubtful still whether there is a single one belonging to the white race" (NR 216–17/145). Through this line, we start to see that what looked like Weil's initial advocacy for civilization has grown more complicated. She is here addressing spiritual and social defects that, in more contemporary terms, would be associated with whiteness. Of the four, she says the false conception of greatness is the most serious.

Weil argues that the false concept of greatness inspired Hitler. According to this concept, to be great is to conquer others. She tasks us with recognizing this concept of greatness still within us; her point is that the idea of national greatness that means dominating others will not simply disappear with the defeat of Hitler. "When we denounce it without the remotest recognition of its application to ourselves," she says in a line that exhibits her sense of humor, "the angels must either cry or laugh, if there happen to be angels who interest themselves in our propaganda" (NR 217/146).[49] "It is chimerical and due to the blindness of national hatred," she goes on, "to imagine that one can exclude Hitler from the title to greatness without a total transformation, among the men of today, of the idea and significance of greatness" (NR 224–25/150). Part of the political task lies with the individual to reorient oneself, for "in order to be able to contribute towards such a transformation, one must have accomplished it in oneself" (NR 225/150). That said, Weil's implicating her readers does not mean that she is offering a self-help manual to an individual (we recall the aforementioned sense of self-becoming that Yountae criticized in favor of an orientation to others). Rather, her focus is on the collectivity. Her argument regards a "total transformation," meaning a reshaping of public life. Her call is for French society to revalue what it understands as great.

* * *

If Weil's critique of greatness anticipates the critical theorists Max Horkheimer and T. W. Adorno's *Dialectic of Enlightenment*, her critique of history echoes Walter Benjamin's "Theses on the Philosophy of History." Her concern is to attend to the history of the underside of the ongoing state of emergency that is European modernity. "The defeated disappear," she says (NR 219/147). "They become naught" (NR 219/147). Focusing on the Roman conquest of Gaul, she challenges the classification "civilizer" in light of how history is told. "[T]he Romans themselves instituted in Gaul and everywhere else the putting to death of thousands of innocent people," she explains, "not in order to do honour to the gods, but in order to amuse the crowds" (NR 220/148). "That was a Roman institution par excellence, one they set up wherever they went; and yet we dare to regard them as civilizers" (NR 220/148). The historiographic problem is that history is "founded upon documents," meaning that historians overlook oral sources and write their own (NR 221/148). The result, Weil concludes in an echo of Benjamin's line that even the dead are not safe from the victor, is a history reliant on force. "History, therefore, is nothing but a compilation of the depositions made by assassins with respect to the victims and themselves" (NR 222/149).

In another point that resonates with her Frankfurt School contemporaries, Weil extends her critique of history to a critique of the normative claim to progress, which she calls a "modern superstition" (NR 227/152). Her main concern is that so-called progress, often meaning the performance of a civilizing mission, uproots other peoples, thereby destroying political, ethical, and spiritual ways of life that could provide an antidote to modern and colonial Europe. Progress, Weil says, "is bound up with the destruction of spiritual treasures of those countries which were conquered by Rome, with the concealment of the perfect continuity existing between these treasures and Christianity, with an historical conception concerning the Redemption, making of the latter a temporal operation instead of an eternal one" (NR 227/152). On this account, progress conflates the supernatural plane with the natural one. It represents the arrogance of uprooted people who in turn uproot others to "redeem" or "save" them. Thus "the idea of progress has become laicized; it is now the bane of our times" (NR 227/152). She goes on: "The dogma of progress brings dishonour upon goodness by turning it into a question of fashion [*une affaire de mode*]" (NR 227/152).

Weil also offers a stunning critique of slavery. She refuses to defend slavery, a refusal in line with abolitionists in our own time. In a long parenthetical in "The Growing of Roots" section of *The Need for Roots*, Weil writes of the Nazis: "Their conception of a just order which is to be the final outcome of their victories rests upon the conviction that, for all who are slaves by nature, servitude is the condition which is at the same time the happiest and the most just" (NR 241/160). Because Aristotle also had a concept of natural slavery, Weil argues that if we adhere to the writings of his followers, such as St. Thomas Aquinas, "even if we reject that particular notion of Aristotle's," she says, "we are necessarily led in our ignorance to accept others which must have lain in him at the root of that one" (NR 241/160). "A man who takes the trouble to draw up an apology for slavery cannot be a lover of justice," she contends (NR 241/160). "The age in which he lived has nothing to do with it" (NR 241/160). And she goes on: "To accept as authoritative the ideas of a man who doesn't love justice constitutes an offence against justice, inevitably punished by a decrease in the powers of discernment" (NR 241/160–61). Because Aristotle recognized that there were debates about slavery in his time, the defense "he was a philosopher of his time" does not hold. Others in his own time criticized the practice of slavery. (Would she extend her critique of slavery to her beloved Plato in the *Republic* and the *Laws*?)

Weil's critique of slavery has immediate and immense implications. In the reform or abolition debates occurring across the United States in regard to policing and prisons, Weil would presumably criticize any reliance on documents written by those who defended slavery. What we often lose when we follow those documents is our capacity to discern what is just. It is here where I think that Weil's severity of analysis and judgment, often criticized as extreme and thus as a weakness of her philosophy, is in fact a strength. If we follow Weil's critique of slavery, then we must overlook the U.S. Constitution and its related jurisprudence in inventing a new social order. Some Indigenous nations in the United States, exemplified in the work of the Lakota People's Law Project, have already been highlighting the need for a new constitution.

Having read her critiques of greatness, history, progress, and slavery, we are not surprised to see Weil subsequently take a jab at those who defend colonization (often in regard to some purported "progress"). Taking a Catholic journal as her object of critique, Weil summarizes: "[I]t said that God had sent Christopher Columbus to America in order that a few centuries later there should be a nation capable of defeating Hitler" (NR 278/183). By this logic, she points out, "God, apparently, also despises races of color: the wholesale extermination of native American peoples in the sixteenth century seemed to him a small price to pay if it meant the salvation of Europeans in the twentieth" (NR 278/183, translation modified). She concludes tongue-in-cheek: "One would have thought that instead of sending Christopher Columbus to America more than four centuries in advance, it would have been simpler to send some one to assassinate Hitler round about the year 1923" (NR 278/184). While this critique, in its economy and tone, ends up showing off Weil's smart sense of humor, the line of reasoning Weil is writing against is no laughing matter. Weil shows here that modern senses of civilization, history, progress, and slavery culminate in the most idiotic, ahistorical, and illogical claims—here that God sent Columbus to defeat Hitler. Such claims, to my mind, provide some evidence to my overall suggestion that perhaps it was not Weil who was crazy but those around her living their "normal" lives.

CRITIQUE OF POLITICAL PARTIES

How Weil theorizes collectivity from London is complicated, in part because she wrote much more than *The Need for Roots*. While in that book she to some extent endorsed the need for collectivity, even a prestigious one, she also maintained some elements of her Platonic critique of collectivity, including in *The Need for Roots* itself:

> Plato found the right expression when he compared the collectivity to an animal. And those who are blinded by its prestige, which means everyone except for a few predestined individuals, "call just and beautiful the things that are necessary, being incapable of discerning and teaching what a distance separates the essence of what is necessary from the essence of what is good." (NR 137)

> Platon a le mot le plus juste en comparant la collectivité à un animal. Et ceux que son prestige aveugle, c'est-à-dire tous les hommes, hors des prédestinés, « appellent justes et belles les choses nécessaires, étant incapables de discerner

et d'enseigner quelle distance il y a entre l'essence du nécessaire et celle du bien. » (NR 95)

With Weil, we could call this conflation, of the necessary with the good, the central conflation of collectivity. Collectivities raise their own power at the expense of the individual. They reorient the individual, such that what the individual considers good and beautiful are aspects of the collective. This reorientation is not esoteric. It occurs in quotidian ways: flags, parades, conventions, barbeques. Justice starts to sound like a procedure completed in a courtroom or through the election of a candidate. The question of finding a truly just balance within social life more broadly is lost or obscured. Thinking disappears.

Weil goes as far as saying that the presence of the collectivity, as the Platonic Great Beast, is so strong that any modern social science must principally consider it: social science "should be founded upon the Platonic notion of the Beast. Social science is the study of the enormous animal and should undertake a minute description of its anatomy, physiology, natural and conditional reflexes, capacity for being broken in" (NR 291/192). And yet, at the end of *Need for Roots*, Weil returns to the question of modern social life, something that stayed with her from at least her 1934 "Reflections" essay. Of "what we call our modern civilization," she continues, "We are very proud of it, but we also know that it is sick. And everybody is agreed about the diagnosis of the sickness. It is sick because it doesn't know exactly what place to give to physical labour and to those engaged in physical labour" (NR 295/196). "It is not difficult to define the place that physical labour should occupy in a well-ordered social life," she continues in the penultimate lines of the book (NR 298/198). "It should be its spiritual core" (NR 298/198). In light of her experience as a worker in factories and in vineyards, she has in mind local organizations, such as cooperative workshops for professions. Importantly, she is at pains to distinguish the root-giving organizations she endorses from forced mechanical labor—what she has in mind are not "small factories [*petites usines*]" (NR 60/47). The workplaces she envisions would operate instead through "organic ties [*liens organiques*]" (NR 60/47). While she concludes *The Need for Roots* with a view toward just collectivities built organically around the needs and duties of individuals who are always imbricated through responsibilities to others, at the same time as she was drafting her long book, she developed a condemnation of a particular form of collectivity in *On the Abolition of All Political Parties*. Reading *On the Abolition of All Political Parties* alongside *The Need for Roots* helps us to understand better Weil's critical/constructive approach to collectivity in the early 1940s.

* * *

In the U.S. context, Weil is known perhaps most for *Waiting for God*, *Gravity and Grace*, and *The Need for Roots*. *On the Abolition of All Political Parties* is a lesser-known work that takes a sharp stance against a form of collectivity Weil deemed totalitarian. It was written at the end of her life, in 1943, and first published seven years later, in February 1950, as *Note sur la suppression générale des partis politiques* in *La Table ronde*. Weil begins *On the Abolition* with contextualization. She is not talking about political parties in a universal sense or in a pan-European sense. Britain, for instance, has a distinct tradition of partisanship, so she will limit her reflections to the Continent and to France in particular. At the time of the 1789 French revolution, she notes, a political party was viewed not as a vehicle for social change toward justice but as a hindrance to such shifts. Quite simply, parties tend toward totalitarianism, a tendency she quoted in the line "One party in power the others in jail" (APP 4/EL 111–12). She then argues against the sunken cost fallacy of those who are comfortable with a static present: "The mere fact that they exist today is not in itself a sufficient reason for us to preserve them. The only legitimate reason for preserving anything is its goodness" (APP 4/EL 112). She notes the criterion for this goodness: "It can only be truth and justice; and, then, the public interest [*l'utilité publique*]" (APP 4/EL 112). The question becomes how the public interest can be in service of the good, and for this she turns to Jean-Jacques Rousseau.

She reads Rousseau's notion of the "general will" somewhat favorably, agreeing with his claim that reason chooses what is just and that reason is shared among people (thus making reason "good" in the above sense regarding public interest, but not necessarily regarding a time-out-of-mind truth). Passions, by contrast, are different. They are contested. As Weil puts it, Rousseau thought that "the general will of a whole nation might in fact conform to justice, for the simple reason that individual passions will neutralise one another and act as mutual counterweights. For him, this was the only reason why the popular will should be preferred to the individual will" (APP 6–7/EL 113). This alignment of reason and cancelling out of passions seems right to Weil, but she notes two further necessary conditions for the general will to be realized. First, "at the time when the people become aware of their own intention and express it, there must not exist any form of collective passion" (APP 7–8/EL 114). When collective passion is at play, passions multiply instead of divide—in this case the individual and not the collective is closer to justice.

"The second condition," she continues, "is that the people should express their will regarding the problems of public life—and not merely choosing among individuals; or, worse, among various irresponsible organizations (for the general will does not have the slightest connection with such choices)"

(APP 9/EL 115). She then returns to 1789 to conclude this point: to the extent that the general will existed then, it was not because it was expressed through partisan elections; rather, it existed precisely because there was something more important than elections, namely, *cahiers de revendications* (statements of grievances). This was a system of expressing public opinion that required listening and compassion. At the same time, the people monitored the representatives to see if their words were interpreted correctly. Such a system, Weil observes, was not to happen again. Instead, we have pretense: "We pretend that our present system is democratic, yet the people never have the chance nor the means to express their views on any problem of public life" (APP 10/EL 115). Her focus on democracy leads to an inquiry into public life; she is especially interested in how questions can be put to the people without their being "infected by collective passions" and thereby avoidant of reason, justice, and goodness (APP 10/EL 116). Hence her central claim: "[I]t appears that any solution will necessarily involve, as the very first step, the abolition of all political parties [*la suppression des partis politiques*]" (APP 11/EL 116).

Weil takes the time to define political parties. They feature, she says, three "essential characteristics": (a) "A political party is a machine to generate collective passions"; (b) "A political party is an organization designed to exert collective pressure upon the minds of all its individual members"; and (c) "The first objective and also the ultimate goal of any political party is its own growth, without limit" (APP 11/EL 116). She adds in the next line: "Because of these three characteristics, every party is totalitarian—potentially, and by aspiration" (APP 11/EL 116). These are all, to different extents, teleological characteristics: a party exists for the purposes of producing collective passions and pressures. Further, it is its own end—or more precisely, its own growth is its own end. As in her early writings, Weil is drawing attention to the fact that the political party reverses means and ends, especially in taking itself as autotelic.[50]

Importantly, the above are *essential* characteristics, by Weil's lights. That is, the teleology of political parties is inherent or fundamental to what they are. As a consequence, it would be a contradiction in terms to advocate for a party that advanced collective reason, for a party that stoked careful thinking instead of persuasive pressure, or for a limited and measured party. These predicates contradict the essence of the political party, on Weil's analysis. It is for this reason—the teleology essential to parties—that it follows that Weil would argue not for reform but for abolition.

Weil spends considerable time elaborating on how political parties are totalitarian in essence. Her argument derives from the third characteristic, namely, a given party's misguided consideration of itself as an end. A party says that it must have power to serve the public interest, but "once obtained, no finite amount of power will ever be deemed sufficient" (APP 14/EL 118). In turn, it tries to gain as much influence as it can both nationally and internationally, such that "the essential tendency of all political parties is toward totalitarianism, first on the national scale then on the global scale" (APP 14/EL 118). "In no circumstance could they ever believe that their party might have too many members, too many votes, too much money" (APP 15/EL 118). In what today we would call a political-theological point, she concludes, "This then amounts to idolatry, for God alone is legitimately his own end" (APP 14/EL 118). She also returns to the first and second essential characteristics.

A party exerts collective pressure through the conformist and ideological pushes of propaganda. Propaganda works "not to impart light but to persuade," and "[a]ll political parties make propaganda" (APP 16/EL 119). A party that thus persuades cannot be good, according to Weil's initial criterion, because to persuade is not to orient others to the truth. While propaganda causes one to perceive some aspects of the party as just and therefore as good, it is selective in its emphasis. One who joins a party based on appreciating its messaging implicitly endorses other party positions with which one is unfamiliar. Thus "he submits his thinking to the authority of the party," and "[a]s later on, little by little, he begins to learn these positions, he will except them without further examination" (APP 27/EL 125). One's identification with the party conditions one's thinking. The attitudinal Rubicon is crossed upon joining the party. The logic of joining is the same that prevents one from thinking later—a submission to authority. "[W]hen a man joins a party, he submissively adopts a mental attitude which he will express later on with words such as 'As a monarchist, as a Socialist, I think that . . .'" (APP 27/EL 125). Individual thinking—on her mind at least since "Prospects"—is lost once again.

The struggle she outlines here is between two perhaps mutually exclusive desires of an individual: the desire to follow an inner goodness in thinking and the desire to act effectively in public affairs.[51] Many students and activists feel this tension today, wondering whether to work "within" or "outside" of "the system" and asking, following Audre Lorde, whether the master's tools can dismantle the master's house. Weil writes, "It would be useless to attempt an escape by establishing a distinction between inner freedom and external discipline, for this would entail lying to the public, towards whom every candidate, every elected representative, has a special duty of truthfulness" (APP 19/EL 121). The problem is that the individual sacrifices her orientation toward inner truth by joining a compromised collectivity. Weil notes that if a member of a political party wanted to pause, step back, and examine an issue with a view solely toward the public interest (and not just the interest of the party), the member would be ridiculed. In fact, she observes incisively, "it seems inconceivable that anyone would dare to utter such words"—that they strive to serve the public and justice (APP 17/EL 120). And yet, "Conversely, everybody feels it is completely natural, sensible and honorable for someone to say, 'As a conservative . . .' or 'As a Socialist, I do think that . . .'" (APP 17/EL 120).

Weil's is a profound comment on the naturalization of collective rationality (a contradiction in terms, for Weil). It also highlights the irony of how someone is in fact considered as *measured* ("sensible") for openly sharing how their thoughts are influenced by an organization that, in essence, is excessive and indeed totalitarian. Finally, it points to the social prestige garnered through such comments, the honor one gets from one's circles when one publicly avows to whom one's thinking belongs. It follows that one who does not preface one's statements with notes of loyalty would be socially constrained.

Weil is remarkably aware of the extent and effect of disciplinary mechanisms not just of political parties but of social life in general. The above thinking, or lack thereof, she says, "is not limited to partisan politics; people are not ashamed to say, 'As a Frenchman, I think that . . .' or 'As a Catholic, I think that . . .'" (APP 18/EL 120). "[T]he party system has painful penalties to chastise insubordination," she writes, and "[t]hese penalties extend into all areas of life: career, affections, friendship, reputation, the external aspect of honour, sometimes even family life" (APP 22/EL 123). Weil's concern—echoing her inquiry in "Reflections" about whether or not all spheres of modern life are poisoned—is that there is not a social sphere that partisan logic does not touch. The intellectual cancer within a party can metastasize, in other words. This is an important point regarding method: with whom we think and what we choose to call into question or to let pass unexamined bear on how we live our lives. Some of these points are simple, such as that one would expect one's reputation to increase when one joins a party or when one dresses "better" (more professionally) at work. Of course there is social reward in those instances. Some of the points are more subtle: the form one's family takes might very well be influenced by "the party line" regarding sexuality and marriage, and even one's affections—one's emotions and attachments—shift due to the social promises and penalties of joining or not joining a party or a collectivity that takes a certain line on regulating sexuality and family life.

Weil's point is that partisan thinking occurs not only in different social spheres (e.g., the family, the workplace) but also in regard to issues in daily conversation. The fact that people analyze social issues without addressing nuance and ambiguity, such that they can only be either for or against a position, Weil writes, is "an exact transposition of the party spirit," which has made its way into literary and artistic circles (APP 32/EL 128). Ultimately, partisan logic is about comfort. "It is so comfortable!" Weil writes, exasperated. "It amounts to having no thoughts at all. Nothing is more comfortable than not having to think" (APP 27/EL 125).Weil concludes her note:

> Nearly everywhere—often even when dealing with purely technical problems—instead of thinking, one merely takes sides: for or against. Such a choice replaces the activity of the mind. This is an intellectual leprosy; it originated in the political world and then spread through the land, contaminating all forms of thinking. This leprosy is killing us; it is doubtful whether it can be cured without first starting with the abolition of political parties. (APP 34)

> Presque partout—et même souvent pour des problèmes purement techniques—l'opération de prendre parti, de prendre position pour ou contre, s'est substituée à l'obligation de la pensée. C'est là une lèpre qui a pris origine dans les milieux politiques, et s'est étendue, à travers tout le pays, presque à la totalité de la pensée. Il est douteux qu'on puisse remédier à cette lèpre, qui nous tue, sans commencer par la suppression des partis politiques. (EL 129)

Weil wrote *On the Abolition* as an occasional piece—in response to the Resistance's question of whether or not to allow for political parties. It remains for us to consider how such a specific piece speaks to our moment of despair today, when many of us intend to resist injustice through participation in some collectivity. What Weil outlines in one of her final essays is the tension of acting in a critical situation with others even when the channels for that action are contaminated—as they always are, being creations of finite and flawed humans. On my reading, it is as if, writing *The Need for Roots* and *On the Abolition of All Political Parties* at the same time, she excised her most damning critiques of collectivity from the former (written with a view toward the regeneration of Europe) and saved them for the latter (written as a polemical critique). If I am right in making that suggestion, then we have yet another example not of unity across space and time in Weil but of a philosopher of plurality, of a mind that evaluates the strengths and limitations of contrary approaches to collective life, and of an intellectual who has the courage to write contrasting essays with a view toward publication. More to the point of this chapter, and in order to think with Weil regarding the possibility of a just collectivity, I will conclude by returning to *The Need for Roots*. The section I want to highlight as of heightened importance today is not her conclusion about the spiritual role of labor but her discussion of community work already underway in times of immense distress.

THE QUESTION OF BELONGING

In the United States today, we remain awash in claims that resonate with the aforementioned Catholic review Weil criticized. In Chicago in July 2020, police defended a statue of Columbus in Grant Park against protestors who tried to take it down. Police injured a friend of mine, a reader of Weil, in that protest. But what bothered him the most, my friend told me afterward, was not the police repression he and others faced but a group of white people having a picnic with a bottle of wine nearby in the park. For them, the police violence against the protestors was a kind of evening entertainment. Activists working to reorient our country's sense of greatness face challenges from not only the police but also from moderates, "reformers," and middle-class citizens who, in their everyday lives, do not take active stands to challenge our false conception of greatness.

In such a context, it is worth reconsidering the fruits of Weil's metaphor of roots. If we scrutinize her concept with the same thoughtful, critical focus she applied to terms such as "revolution," and if we do so for our own context, as she was always doing in hers, what might we gain? Reading Weil through Arendt, Mary Dietz has argued that Weil's metaphor is limited because it suggests an organic process as opposed to a need for human activity. On this reading, the value of the metaphor of roots is that it "gets us to recognize ourselves as creatures who need stability, permanence, and security in order to grow and flourish, and as collective beings whose societies are complex and dynamic living wholes, cultural 'root systems,' as it were."[52] Dietz points out that a concept borrowed from the natural world leads to further descriptions of politics as akin to nature: a healthy society involves growth, nourishment, fertile soil, and elemental balance. We can expect societies to have a life-cycle, to grow and decay. "Weil's metaphor works to remind us of what humans share with nature," Dietz goes on—"Like plants, our societies are at once sturdy and fragile; we can escape neither the rhythm of the seasons nor the forces of disintegration, whether natural or human."[53]

"But there is something incomplete about this metaphor, and, accordingly, about a political perspective that takes its inspiration from the literal idea of roots and rootedness," Dietz begins her critique of the term. "For despite what they share with the natural realm, human societies are also vastly different from the culture-bed of plant forms or the vital mediums of organic life."[54] Because humans are political animals, "to ascribe organic characteristics to humans as political beings, or to analyze political matters in terms of biological metaphors, is to diminish, if not altogether destroy, the special meaning and the distinctiveness of the political itself."[55] For Dietz, what political readers gain from studying Weil's metaphor of roots in regard to political life is outweighed by what is lost if the image is taken too far. "[B]y ascribing biological characteristics to political phenomena," Dietz concludes,

> [Weil] fails to plumb the depths of the very political phenomena (such as "politics," "country," and "citizenship") she is intent upon preserving. Indeed, if we were to push her organic metaphor to its farthest limit, we might be inclined to view politics, country, and citizenship as parts of a causal and cyclical life-process that, somehow, determines human life and can neither be radically altered nor rearranged.[56]

Ultimately, for Dietz, Weil's metaphors in *The Need for Roots* "leave too much out. The idea of country as a 'culture-bed' or of patriotism as the right sort of love toward the 'roots' that sustain us, do not sufficiently emphasize that human beings are actors and creators of the world, not simply organic objects in it."[57]

Dietz's critique carries considerable insight: the central limitation to applying organic metaphors to the political realm is their implication of a natural process, suggesting that politics is part of a series of events that happens in cycles anyway. In one register, we can hear Dietz as reading Arendt, with her stress on action and new creation in public and plurality, against Weil's stress on the organic and historical playing out in private. Dietz's reading is a helpful corrective, then; it prevents the reader from taking Weil's metaphor of roots to a place where the ruling class naturalizes a political order.[58] Indeed, the organic metaphor of roots is perhaps most problematic in suggesting a pre-political realm of belonging, here to a country. "Radical discourses and practices that seek to overcome coloniality," Rinaldo Walcott writes, "might want to refuse the logics of belonging to place, in the sense of past ownership or claim to land, and instead forge a relational logic with Fanon's landless 'damned of the earth.'"[59] Walcott continues: "Such a claim is not to ignore that human beings need to belong; rather, it is to position belonging outside its historical, naturalized, quasi-organic trajectory and to create another form of sociability not premised on a history of racist social, political, and cultural gradations and exclusion."[60] Here readers of Weil might, once again, want to read Weil against herself.

In her notebooks Weil writes, "We must be rooted in the absence of place" (GG 39/45). If we are to look to her theological writings to respond to Dietz's and others' critiques of Weil's organic metaphor of roots, we must also note that in those writings Weil does *not* prescribe what Walcott endorsed as a "relational logic." She says explicitly, "Rootedness lies in something other than the social" (GG 169/163). Supplementing her notebooks with her essay "Human Personality," we find the answer to our question about where, if not the social, Weil places roots. In a memorable passage, she writes, "It is the light falling continually from heaven which alone gives a tree energy to send powerful roots deep into the earth. The tree is really rooted in the sky" (SWA 86/EL 27). "It is only what comes from heaven," Weil goes on, "that can make a real impress on the earth" (SWA 86/EL 27). "By saying the tree is really rooted in the sky," Sarah MacMillen comments on Gillian Rose's use of Weil's line, "she is saying that those things that bespeak gravity, logic, and politics, are not divorced from spiritual and religious life."[61] MacMillen concludes: "Suspension in the sky of transcendence is without affirming a fixed identity."[62] Perhaps as readers of Weil we need at least one figure of remove, here through Rose, in order to bring Weil's lines about supernatural roots back to earth. What Walcott's above lines help us see is how necessary it is today to find a sense of belonging precisely in the social, in forms of solidarity instead of in biological ties. To read Weil's political promise in tension with her organic metaphor of roots, I will not look to her personal theological reflections but instead stay with her political writings written with a clear goal and to a known audience. In what is left of this chapter, I read a portion of "The Growing of Roots" for its emphasis on humans as actors and creators. There is a moment in *The Need for Roots* where Weil says the creation of a new collectivity requires the skill of an artist. It is in this moment that I find the most political promise with respect to responding to our context of occupied cities today.

TOWARD A NEW POLITY

Noting that several nascent political organizations already existed in 1943 France, Weil says they "must be examined, viewed on the spot, and the authority emanating from London must be used like a tool to shape them discretely and patiently, like a sculptor who divines the shape contained in the block of marble in order to bring it forth" (NR 212/142). In this discussion of shaping political organizations in France, she affirms once again the role of collectivity:

> An organization which can crystallize and seize upon the words launched officially, translate their inspiration into different words entirely of its own, realize them in coordinated actions for which it offers an ever-increasing guarantee of efficacity; can be a living, warm environment, full of friendly intercourse, companionship, and kindness—that is the sort of humus in which the unfortunate French, uprooted by the disaster, can live and find their salvation both in war and in peace. (NR 212/142)

Weil's metaphors remain organic and theological. France is to grow in the humus of collectivity and thereby find salvation. But it is a particular kind of salvation that she has in mind, and in specifying her term she returns her reader not to a supernatural realm but to the daily practices previously and already occurring on the ground in France.

> The unique source of salvation and greatness for France lies in regaining contact with her genius in the depths of her distress. This must be accomplished now, immediately; whilst the distress is still a crushing one; whilst France still has before her, in the future, the opportunity of making real the first conscious glimmerings of her recovered genius by expressing them through warlike action. (NR 212/142)

It is tempting here to focus on her concluding call for war. And she elaborates on what she means, noting that "[a]fter victory" the opportunity for inspiration would be lost, so first "France must once more be fully present in this war, share in the victory at the cost of her blood" (NR 213/142). But she qualifies her claims. "The true mission of the French movement in London," she concludes, "is, by reason even of the military and political circumstances, a spiritual mission before being a military and political one. It could be defined as being that of director of conscience on a national plane" (NR 213/143). And she goes on to liken the kind of political concentration necessary to fulfill the prescriptions in *The Need for Roots* to "that required for creative work in art or science" (NR 213/143). Indeed, she asks, "[W]hy should politics, which decide the fate of peoples and whose object is justice, demand any less concentration than art or science, whose respective objects are beauty and truth?" (NR 213/143).

It is here that I find Weil so worthwhile to read in the present. She suggests that in a context of occupation, the political task is to come into contact with "genius in the depths of . . . distress." This is a creative task akin to making art. Yes, Weil's argument lends itself to the claim that in uprootedness, the only reality lies in the past and the future. She writes, "France's only reality today consists in memories and hopes" (NR 101/73). But in lines such as the aforementioned, which set the task as attuning oneself to creativity under constraint, I read her as pointing us to the present as well as, importantly, to public life. Even in a context of general uprootedness, there are those who are working to grow roots.

On my reading, we need to recognize that when Weil compares politics to art, she is writing about the collective, not individual, level. Too much of a focus on Weil's spiritual biography functions to suggest that her politics is best understood as idiosyncratic individual action. I think that is misguided. To conclude this chapter, I will place Weil in dialogue with political theorists

Jodi Dean and Adolph Reed Jr. This dialogue demonstrates that Weil maintained a revisionist Marxism throughout her life, especially in her ongoing commitment to raising consciousness in French publics through her occasional writings and through her continual organizing among workers. It also allows me to argue that Weil's critique of the idolatry of the self, coupled with her promotion of collectivity in *The Need for Roots*, results in a political philosophy that is looking for what Reed would call a movement. We do not necessarily need to read Weil's notebooks to understand that she thinks placing the private self at the center of politics is an error. As I have tried to show in this chapter, we can also see it in the way she frames the problematic of *The Need for Roots*.

WEIL'S CONTRIBUTIONS TO PUBLIC LIFE

In *Between the Human and the Divine*, Dietz argues that Weil's antidote to national uprootedness and its perpetuation lies in the private sphere. On Dietz's reading, Weil outlines a political strategy under conditions of uprootedness that uses "checks that exist in the private realm to counter the excesses of individual behavior and encourage civility and fairness toward others" while discarding "hindrances in an uprooted public, where the more excessive one's pride in the nation, the better."[63] If we follow Dietz, we would worry that Weil's prescriptions of practices that I outlined in the chapter on the neoliberal self, such as contemplation in solitude, coupled with a critique of an uprooted citizenry, tacitly support the neoliberal gutting of public life. In response to this objection, and by way of conclusion, I inquire into Weil's suggestions for how a collectivity needs to grow roots, and I highlight the public checks she offers.

To begin our inquiry into how Weil theorizes public life, we can return to terrain we've already crossed. Weil's critique of money and the nation-state as uprooting diagnose what political theorist Bonnie Honig calls the anti-public "consumer need" for private objects, "the fetish [that] is more like the ruin, the remnant, of the democratic desire to constellate affectively around shared objects, public things."[64] It is true that in *The Need for Roots* Weil is not making an explicit defense of public parks, schools, water, transportation systems, and so on, even if she hints, only one paragraph after describing the need for roots, at the importance of museums (the translation says "picture gallery" instead of her original *un musée*) as an analogy for other needed social environments (NR 40/36).[65] However, Weil does outline the psychological or spiritual necessary conditions for a citizenry to reject full-scale privatization (a misorientation) and cultivate a new collectivity, what with Honig we might call a new public. It is by theorizing in regard to this more fundamental level that Weil also speaks of building a political movement required to carry out the collective (public) promise of individuals' new orientations.

In theorizing a sense of political belonging for the present, Jodi Dean advances a return to the idea of the comrade. "Under conditions where political change seems completely out of reach," she writes diagnostically, "we might imagine political work as self-transformation. At the very least, we can work on ourselves."[66] Like Weil, Dean is deeply critical of thinking of politics primarily as work on yourself. Dean's critique of self-work in her book *Comrade* emerges in her discussion of the contemporary language of allyship. "Generally, allies are privileged people who want to do something about oppression. They may not consider themselves survivors or victims, but they want to help . . . Allies don't want to image themselves as homophobic, racist, or sexist. They see themselves as the good guys, part of the solution."[67] "Like eliminate-the-clutter books or tips for clean eating," Dean continues, "the instructions for being a good ally are mini lifestyle manuals, techniques for navigating the neoliberal environment of privilege and oppression. Individuals can learn what not to say and what not to do. They can feel engaged, changing their feelings if not the world without taking power, without any organized political struggle at all."[68] The ally moves primarily through three terrains: posting on social media, contributing to charities, and conversing with others.[69] Dean's concern is that these terrains don't lead to a social movement or institutions that can effectuate real political change. We learn all the right terms, all the right words, what to say and what not to say, and then we feel satisfied, engaged, perhaps even radical—at the very least, we feel *political*. But for Dean this feeling is meaningless without a political institution such as a party. This is the key difference between Dean's and Weil's Marxism: Dean strongly advocates for a party. But their sphere of agreement is larger than that of disagreement.

Dean says in a critique, "[A]llyship is a disposition, a confrontation not with state or capitalist power but with one's own discomfort."[70] She sees this disposition as shrinking the political sphere, meaning that what counts as political action becomes limited to social media and yourself. Both are individuating, exemplified in Googling things yourself and wearing different clothes. We consume information and educate ourselves instead of organizing social life with others. And we might be scolded or shamed if we do not educate ourselves properly. Weil would have severe reservations about such an individuated politics. Her call for the mission of the Free French to act as a national conscience assumes the need for collective education and action, not an individual refashioning.

For Dean, if we want to maintain our individualistic stance on politics, and if we think we have a unique viewpoint in a world where the internet and advertising greatly condition our preferences and tastes and desires that we nevertheless call our own, then we are already caught in capitalist thinking: we want to be individuated, unique, different, and ultimately better than someone else.[71] And so if we think about self-transformation, we think about looking differently—a new look, a new fashion, a new you. Dean is not proposing self-transformation. Rather, she is proposing discipline, joy, enthusiasm, and courage.[72] The way to move from being an ally to being a comrade is to take a side not on social media or with your friends or family but in a larger context. We might organize a union or support a new political party. For Dean, the comrade also involves a set of expectations. Unlike the ally who leaves the struggle when things get difficult or when the group makes a decision they can't stomach, the comrade sticks around (as Weil did, seen in her ardent desire to return to London, which can be understood not as wanting to suffer with others but as wanting to stand alongside them). Comrades surrender some of their individual autonomy for the sake of a larger direction of the collective.

In a choice of words that is mostly excised in Wills's translation, Weil in fact uses the language of comradeship in *The Need for Roots*. Wills maintains the language only in Weil's marginal discussion of Felix Le Dantec and Bonnot (NR 236/157). But Weil describes the re-rooting of the working class in terms of little workshops that develop bonds of comradery [*liens de camaraderie*] (NR 73/55). She also discusses how, in her uprooted context, commercial forces have triumphed over working-class comradery [*la camaraderie ouvrière*] (NR 124/87). In making an analogy between a miner who gives everything to his fellow workers and a citizen who feels an obligation to their country, she writes that the miner responds knowing that his comrades are in danger of death [*des camarades en péril de mort*] (NR 158/107). And perhaps most importantly, after a paragraph claiming that a number of religious and resistance organizations become corpses if they get co-opted by state institutions of public administration, she admits that "if associations of this sort are out of contact with public affairs [*la vie publique*], they cease to exist" (NR 165/112). "It is necessary, therefore," she concludes, "that while not forming part of the administration, they should yet at the same time not lose all contact with it" (NR 165/112). When she discusses how this minimal contact would function, she describes state-chosen, temporary representatives. These comrades, she says, would have to understand their selection as a matter of honor [*tous leurs camarades y trouvent un motif de fierté*] (NR 165/112). Such an institution could function only if it maintained internal differences. "In a country like ours," Weil continues, "the perpetual stirring of ideas can never do any harm. It is mental inertia which is fatal to it" (NR 165/112). At the very least, even if Weil would remain suspicious of political parties, her endorsement of comradeship suggests that she would've been in favor of what María Lugones and others now talk about in terms of the coalition.[73]

Weil's link between comradeship and institutional transformation is important. If we start from Weil's private notebooks and study her biography in relation to her relationship to religion, then we find a politics focused on private life and individual orientation and transformation. This is to read Weil as a cultural theorist who emphasizes quotidian, private acts of resistance. And in this view, as Adolph Reed Jr. comments, "If all is resistance, there is no need for concerning with mobilizing collective action, especially because in this view public institutions are inauthentic or corrupting."[74] Indeed, if we read Weil only as a critic of collectivity, and one who focuses on the right orientation of the individual, then to follow her could be to exhibit what Reed calls "a preference for strategies of 'resistance' to imperatives of institutions and 'transgression' of conventions rather than strategies aimed at transformation of institutions and social relations."[75] But if we start from her meant-for-publication writings and study her life for how she essayed those ideas in the world, then we allow ourselves to learn from a political philosopher who is more focused on public actions than our initial glance let us see.

Reed offers an alternative to private strategies of resistance and transgression. This strategy for building "the movement we need," he says, "can be built only through connecting with large numbers of people in cities and towns and workplaces all over the country who can be brought together around a political agenda that speaks directly and clearly to their needs and aspirations as they perceive them."[76] Like Weil, he focuses on needs. "We can create it," he elaborates later, "only through direct organizing and mobilization within the class, at the level of the neighborhood, the workplace and the union, and it can be created only by recognizing that it does not yet exist."[77] "A truly popular politics of this stripe," he concludes, "cannot be built, especially not in its early stages, mainly through big events. It grows much more from one-on-one interaction and with small groups of coworkers, neighbors, friends and other associates."[78]

I suggest that we can read *The Need for Roots* as following Reed's strategy. It starts from the needs of the soul and from conversations across the working class, and it then addresses different contexts across France—towns, countryside, and the nation as a whole. Weil's political biography—working in Parisian factories, organizing labor while she was a teacher, spreading literature for the Free French, and speaking with migrants in Marseilles—reads as a test-case of Reed's call for "direct organizing." By *The Need for Roots*, her critique of collectivity looks less like she is against collective life *per se* and more like she is advancing a plan for small-scale interactions as opposed to large events and rallies. The early stages of post-occupation political life she is advancing, I am suggesting, are in line with Reed's call; they outline public organizing more than private actions.

In sum, my argument is that *The Need for Roots* offers foundational modes for reorienting public life. It is not an argument for specific public goods, such as parks and libraries. But its suggestions could be worth taking on for living out a meaningful sense of political responsibility, one that includes artistic dispositions toward a collective past, present, and future. These artistic dispositions refuse to center their lives on the abstractions of money, the nation-state, and the related conception of greatness as forceful conquest of others. If a society is to regain or maintain a flourishing public life, then its citizens need to cultivate these dispositions. A careful reading of *The Need for Roots* allows us to see the spirit of comradeship Weil offers. At times this spirit reads as a resuscitation of nationalism and private individualism; and sometimes this is simply the case. But by and large, when the text appears to be insufficiently radical, it is simply starting from the needs of its audience as they perceive them. From there, Weil initiates a critical conversation about the values of the polity, showing her reader how to connect their conceptions to public consequences and thus demonstrating the need for revaluations of greatness. And so it is in *The Need for Roots*, I am arguing, that Weil's method of starting from the position of the oppressed, her critique of colonialism, her call for a reorientation of the self and the polity, and her critique of rights come together—not seamlessly or even always coherently but in a way that allows her to side against her previous claims and to grapple with what she had written even on previous pages. Read thus, *The Need for Roots* demonstrates not a simple unity but one philosopher's ongoing and inspiring struggle with a contradictory and unjust reality. What follows from such an inquiry remains, returning to Dietz, what we might call the need for action.

NOTES

1. Katie Galioto, "As Chauvin Verdict Looms, Military Presence in Twin Cities Unsettles Some, Reassures Others," *Star Tribune*, April 19, 2021, https://www.startribune.com/as-chauvin-verdict-looms-military-presence-in-twin-cities-unsettles-some-reassures-others/600047529/?refresh=true. Accessed May 5, 2021.

2. Alicia Eler, "Two Young Artists Create a 'Cemetery' in Minneapolis to Honor Victims of Police Killings," *Star Tribune*, June 12, 2020, https://www.startribune.com/two-young-artists-create-a-cemetery-in-minneapolis-to-honor-victims-of-police-killings/571213142/. Accessed May 5, 2021.

3. Sheila Nezhad, "Minneapolis Doesn't Need a National Guard Occupation," *Star Tribune*, February 28, 2021, https://www.startribune.com/minneapolis-doesn-t-need-a-national-guard-occupation/600028732/. Accessed May 5, 2021.

4. Shawn Manke, "Minnesota National Guard is Here to Protect People, Their Rights and Their Property," *Star Tribune*, March 7, 2021, https://www.startribune .com/minnesota-national-guard-is-here-to-protect-people-their-rights-and-their -property/600031568/?refresh=true. Accessed May 5, 2021.

5. Faiza Mahamud, "Among Minnesota's Refugees, Military Presence in Twin Cities Stirs Painful Memories," *Star Tribune*, April 22, 2021, https://www.startribune .com/among-minnesota-s-refugees-military-presence-in-twin-cities-stirs-painful -memories/600048897/?refresh=true. Accessed May 5, 2021.

6. Bernard Harcourt, *The Counterrevolution: How Our Government Went to War Against Its Own Citizens* (New York: Basic Books, 2018), 8.

7. See ibid.

8. Here I am trying not to fall into the idea that there would be an easy "after" occupation. I thank Helen Kinsella for drawing my attention to this point. I also borrow the formulation of "in the wake" from Christina Sharpe. See Christina Sharpe, *In the Wake: On Blackness and Being* (Durham, NC: Duke University Press, 2016).

9. On September 10, 1942, Weil wrote to Thibon that the idea of this corps of nurses "[s]eems to me to have been sent me by God" (Pétrement, *Simone Weil*, 480). Cha reads the corps as giving us a "concrete example of doing nothing and everything out of love—a generosity, we might say, that is underwritten by the destitution of a self left behind" (Cha, *Decreation*, 105).

10. Pétrement, *Simone Weil*, 477.

11. McLellan, *Utopian Pessimist*, 223.

12. Pétrement, *Simone Weil*, 477.

13. Ibid.

14. Rinaldo Walcott, *The Long Emancipation: Moving Toward Black Freedom* (Durham, NC: Duke University Press, 2021), 5.

15. Ibid.

16. Pétrement, *Simone Weil*, 482; McLellan, *Utopian Pessimist*, 232.

17. McLellan, *Utopian Pessimist*, 228.

18. Pétrement, *Simone Weil*, 487.

19. Ibid., 490–91.

20. McLellan, *Utopian Pessimist*, 245. See also Cha's footnote about Weil's work as a *rédactrice* in Cha, *Decreation*, 159.

21. Pétrement, *Simone Weil*, 512.

22. McLellan, *Utopian Pessimist*, 260.

23. Ibid., 529. Weil participated, among doing other things, by delivering the *Cahiers du Témoignage Chrétien* in the French Free Zone; this paper encouraged the French to resist cooperating with the Nazis and their occupation (Doering, *Simone Weil*, 61).

24. Walter D. Mignolo, *The Darker Side of the Renaissance: Literacy, Territoriality, and Colonization* (Ann Arbor: University of Michigan Press, 1995), 5.

25. Antonio Y. Vázquez-Arroyo, *Political Responsibility: Responding to Predicaments of Power* (New York: Columbia University Press, 2016), 240.

26. Christy Wampole, *Rootedness: The Ramifications of a Metaphor* (Chicago: University of Chicago Press, 2016), 132.

27. Shannon Hoff, "Rights and Worlds: On the Political Significance of Belonging," *Philosophical Forum* 45, no. 4 (2014).

28. Ibid., 356.

29. Ibid.

30. Ibid., 362.

31. Wampole, *Rootedness*, 2.

32. Ibid.

33. Ibid., 4.

34. An Yountae, *The Decolonial Abyss: Mysticism and Cosmopolitics from the Ruins* (New York: Fordham University Press, 2016), 105.

35. Ibid.

36. Scott Ritner explains how Weil offers a pedagogy of self-transformation that is different from the neoliberal emphasis on self-becoming: "The relationship between affliction and attention is generated by the underlying practice of discipline. The training of the soul has the dialectical possibilities of oppression and liberation that depends not only on the orientation—though that is of great import—but also on the quality of the training, the space in which the training takes place (prison, factory, or fields), and the methods used to convey discipline to the trainees (cadence, rhythm) . . . The orientation of attention toward the world, rather than the self, provides the pathway toward a free form of labor and a free form of life. Nonetheless, the development of attentive capacities requires its own form of training" (Scott B. Ritner, "The Training of the Soul: Simone Weil's Dialectical Disciplinary Paradigm, A Reading alongside Michel Foucault," in *Simone Weil and Continental Philosophy*, ed. A. Rebecca Rozelle-Stone [New York: Rowman & Littlefield International, 2017], 200).

37. For a reading of the *pueblo* as a radical political category, see Dussel, *Twenty Theses*. For my reading of Dussel's *pueblo* in connection to responsibilities, see Benjamin P. Davis, "Responsibilities of the Intellectual: Dewey, Dussel, and Democracy," *Inter-American Journal of Philosophy* 11, no. 2 (2020): 35–48.

38. See Kaia Hubbard, "Outside of Sleeping, Americans Spend Most of Their Time Watching Television," *U.S. News*, July 22, 2021, https://www.usnews.com/news/best-states/articles/2021-07-22/americans-spent-more-time-watching-television-during-covid-19-than-working. It is arguable that part of the reason we (in the U.S.) do not understand our own imperial history, on "our" continent and beyond, is that we distract ourselves constantly with our devices.

39. See Nicola Perugini and Neve Gordon, *The Human Right to Dominate* (New York: Oxford, 2015), 1.

40. Stuart Hall, "Racism and Reaction," in *Selected Political Writings*, eds Sally Davison et al. (Durham, NC: Duke University Press, 2017), 143.

41. Ibid., 150.

42. Ibid., 151.

43. Radzins, "Simone Weil's Social Philosophy," 70.

44. Ibid., 71.

45. Dietz, *Between*, 168.

46. Ibid., 162.

47. Édouard Glissant, *Poetics of Relation*, trans. Betsy Wing (Ann Arbor: University of Michigan Press, 1997), 13.

48. Ibid.

49. It is exceedingly rare to come across a reading of Weil that considers not her sense of humor, but even that she had a sense of humor. I hope that my suggestion in this book that Weil is a fellow-traveler, a human like the rest of us, will lead to some readings that consider the multifaceted parts of her personality, including her idiosyncratic humor.

50. This, she says, is a feature not just of political parties but "it is a particular instance of the phenomenon which always occurs whenever thinking individuals are dominated by a collective structure—a reversal of the relation between ends and means" (APP 11–12). And she extends this inversion generally in modern life: "Everywhere, without exception, all the things that are generally considered ends are in fact, by nature, by essence, and in a most obvious way, mere means. One could cite countless examples of this from every area of life: money, power, the state, national pride, economic production, universities, etc., etc." (APP 12/116–17).

51. She comments later, "When a country has political parties, sooner or later it becomes impossible to intervene effectively in public affairs without joining a party and playing the game. Whoever is concerned for public affairs will wish his concern to bear fruit. Those who care about the public interest must either forget their concern and turn to other things, or submit to the grind of the parties. In the latter case, they shall experience worries that will soon supersede their original concern for the public interest" (APP 24/123–24).

52. Dietz, *Between*, 184.

53. Ibid.

54. Ibid.

55. Ibid., 185.

56. Ibid.

57. Ibid.

58. It is worth remembering that, like readers of Hegel, readers of Weil are found on both the Left and the Right. On the troubling way Laurent Wauquiez, the leader of France's largest conservative party, the Republicans, cited *The Need for Roots* as his favorite book, Robert Zaretsky comments, "If Weil's admirers feel an affinity with Weil, it's only because they are misreading her work and her vision of a properly rooted France and Europe" (Robert Zaretsky, "France's Far-Right Claims a Left-Anarchist Martyr as Its Own," *Foreign Policy*, accessed May 2021, https://foreignpolicy.com/2018/07/30/frances-far-right-claims-a-left-anarchist-martyr-as-its-own/). And Christy Wampole has recently reminded us readers of Weil to keep in mind "the overlap of nationalism and ecology," especially given that "[t]he most evil acts in twentieth-century Europe were precipitated by root thinking" (Wampole, *Rootedness*, 3, 123). Alain Finkielkraut is another example of a contemporary French writer enlisting Weil in the service of writing against immigration.

59. Walcott, *The Long Emancipation*, 67.

60. Ibid.

61. Sarah MacMillen, "Faith Beyond Optimism: Simone Weil, Hannah Arendt, and Gillian Rose," *Philosophy and Theology* 23, no. 2 (2011): 264.

62. Ibid., 265.

63. Dietz, *Between*, 162.

64. Bonnie Honig, *Public Things: Democracy in Disrepair* (New York: Fordham University Press, 2017), 31.

65. But doesn't her call for a spiritual (and not simply a legal) education for judges raise problems in countries with a separation of church and state? See NR 38/35.

66. Jodi Dean, *Comrade: An Essay on Political Belonging* (New York: Verso, 2019), 8.

67. Ibid., 16.

68. Ibid., 17.

69. Ibid.

70. Ibid., 18.

71. Ibid., 93.

72. Ibid., 85.

73. See María Lugones, *Pilgrimages/Peregrinajes: Theorizing Coalition against Multiple Oppressions* (Lanham: Rowman & Littlefield, 2003).

74. Adolph Reed Jr., *Class Notes: Posing as Politics and Other Thoughts on the American Scene* (New York: New Press, 2001), xxvi.

75. Ibid., xiv.

76. Ibid., viii–ix.

77. Ibid., xxviii.

78. Ibid.

Conclusion

From Theory to Practice

The Left in the United States today has not overcome the tensions it faced at the end of the twentieth century. In his 1992 *In Theory*, Marxist Aijaz Ahmad observed that post-1968 "theory" displaced "an activist culture" with "a textual culture."[1] Commenting on Ahmad, in her 1996 *Resisting State Violence*, political philosopher Joy James argued that in the academy "conversation deradicalizes as it inbreeds."[2] And in his 2000 *Class Notes*, political theorist Adolph Reed Jr. diagnosed a Left "flight from concreteness."[3] "[I]n what passes for a left public sphere," Reed writes, "there is little sense of creating a movement as an activity that rests on organizing, working actually to build support and solidarity among real people in real places around concrete objectives that they perceive as concerns."[4] Reed reminds his reader that these real people "may not, indeed probably do not, all start from commitment to what is generally understood as a left political perspective or identification with issues that leftists see as highly symbolic."[5]

Reed locates reasons why the Left, by the turn of the century, did not work sufficiently to organize ordinary people in "structuralist Marxism" as well as in "interpretive programs and intellectual sensibilities represented by such labels as poststructuralism, deconstruction, and postmodernism."[6] For their part, structuralist Marxists "failed to see the processual, dialectical character of political action, its contingent open-endedness."[7] Drawing on Marx's famous line from *The Eighteenth Brumaire*—that people make history, but in conditions not of their own making—Reed argues that structuralists focused too much on the latter, on how people are determined by forces outside of them. Like Weil's, his analysis is attuned to class position; he argues that the "almost sentimental pessimism" of structuralist Marxists is little more than a "highly theorized retreat to a world-weary, sometimes agonizedly disappointed quietism that presumes the privilege of secure, middle to upper-middle class employment with good benefits."[8]

If the structuralists retreat through overemphasizing large forces, the poststructuralists reject attempts to build power through over-theorizing small forces. In poststructuralism Reed sees "a focus on the supposedly liberatory significance of communities and practices defined by their marginality in relation to systems of entrenched power or institutions" and "a preference for strategies of 'resistance' to imperatives of institutions and 'transgression' of conventions rather than strategies aimed at transformation of institutions and social relations."[9] He also notes poststructuralists' general suspicion of truth and power, which leads to a retreat into identities.

For Reed, the biggest problem with the poststructuralist move to read the social world as a text is that it implies the reverse, namely, that reading a text differently can change the world.[10] "This reversal is an attractive fiction," he observes, "partly because it invests studies of literary and other forms of cultural production with an aura of political importance they would not otherwise possess."[11] Thus, long days writing at our computers get conflated with political action—a conflation that reaches a "point of solipsism."[12] Simply put, Reed concludes, in no way are "the practices of textual interpretation or the production and analysis of forms of popular culture" equal to "direct challenges to power relations," such as a strike, an electoral victory, a mobilization to honor a treaty, or winning national healthcare.[13]

Perhaps the worst part of the academic turn to poststructuralism is how we academics treat one another. To be understood as a rigorous theorist today too often means remaining within the norms Reed observed twenty years ago: "Pursuit of respectability in mainstream academic disciplines required shelving the idea of class struggle as an orienting principle of inquiry and debate."[14] It is not a coincidence that the uprooted lives of many major theorists—traveling from continent to continent to give papers, conduct workshops, and present their research—leaves little time for local struggle, including labor organization at their own universities. As Weil teaches us, uprooted individuals perpetuate uprootedness. Accordingly, a high theorist might show his graduate students the instabilities of claims to power while not showing up for the students' attempt to form a union. If he is to sketch a political vision, it is likely not to be built around what Reed calls "a coherent common program" but instead around "constructing and imposing formal images of representativeness."[15] What results is a political scene that is "fundamentally counter-solidaristic," with a "default posture" of accusation and a motivation by "[the] presumption of others' bad faith."[16]

Through nearly one quarter of the twenty-first century, scholarship across the humanities and social sciences has yet to overcome the "textual culture" Ahmad, James, and Reed diagnose. Legal theorist Bernard Harcourt, in his 2020 *Critique and Praxis*, identifies lasting problems resonant with those the above authors point out. For Harcourt, following the "collapse of Soviet communism, the eclipse of the student and worker revolts of May 1968, [and] the hegemonic emergence of global neoliberalism," critical theory "took an epistemological detour and moved away from praxis."[17] This detour was, he maintains, reasonable—"a necessary corrective to the know-it-all intellectual telling everyone what they should do."[18] But instead of generating a "productive debate over praxis," the turn to epistemology led to "a further withdrawal of critical philosophy into the academy," narrowing "[t]he space of critique" to "effete universities and colleges."[19] Harcourt's recent critique shows not only that the textual culture remains, but also that it is taken seriously as a problem not just by three theorists with varying commitments to Marxism but also by someone who centers Nietzsche and Foucault. The predicament is so dire that Harcourt can announce "[t]he collapse of critical philosophy" in the present.[20] "Critique is failing at the time it is needed most," he argues, "producing a real crisis in critical theory itself."[21]

Simone Weil did not overstate what reading texts differently could achieve politically. Following Marx, yes, she wrote to clarify the wishes and the struggles of her age; but she never stopped there. Going further, she tested her ideas through practice—on factory floors, in the Spanish Civil War, in Marseilles courtrooms, alongside workers in Harlem, and in dialogue with other exiles in London. It is her dual sense of "essay" that I invoke by noting, in conclusion, the need to connect theory to practice (thus affirming a separation between the two). To write is first to interpret the world. Usually it takes an inflated sense of oneself to claim that one's writing itself changes the world. W. E. B. Du Bois, Claudia Jones, and Frantz Fanon could fairly make this point (and yet for each of them organizing and action remained central). But for the rest of us, one insight Weil offers critical theorists today is an acknowledgment of the limits of theory. She reminds us that writing always needs to be essayed—to be tested in the world. With Weil's reminder and example in mind, political philosophy today can reorient itself toward an activist culture.

In the late 1920s, Weil had few friends at the prestigious École Normale. Her peers interpreted her persistent questioning and polemical, unpatriotic political positions as demonstrating a lack of social skills. It did not help that she was always asking her fellow students for their signatures on left-wing petitions as well as for financial contributions in support of trade-union strikes or to donate to the unemployed. For her first teaching post, she requested a port or industrial town in northern or central France (so as to be close to Paris). Her request was denied, and she was appointed to Le Puy. Her time there is instructive. In late 1931 she worked to consolidate working-class groups, including Communists.[22] Her commitment as an activist included accompanying the unemployed to city council meetings and spending time with working men in cafés. Many people in Le Puy frowned upon her actions, especially given that she was a woman and thus crossed the norm to keep genders separate in public. As a consequence, she was threatened with potential dismissal from her teaching post.[23] Weil's dismissal was avoided, however, in part due to the urging of students in her philosophy class to have their parents sign a petition in support of her.[24] The teachers' union she had joined also defended her.[25] In addition, Weil wrote on behalf of the Committee of the Unemployed of Le Puy. On January 22, 1932, *La Tribune* published her communiqué, which stated, "Between the unemployed and the ruling class there are only relations of force."[26] In response to Weil's activism, the Parisian weekly *Le Charivari* made reference to her as a Jewess and accused her of being "a militant of Moscow."[27] Yet at this time, Weil wrote in a letter to her parents, she was, in fact, becoming less and less a communist, even as she taught a course on Karl Marx to workers.[28] In this decision we see once again the lively, active tensions between Weil's lifelong commitment to Marxian thought and her equally persistent skepticism toward collectivities, including political parties.

Looking to early Weil, we gain a political path forward. Even as Weil became less and less a communist, even as her theoretical reservations to a communist program mounted, and even as she articulated a more precise need for theory and analysis to come *before* revolutionary action, she organized labor. Her organization resulted in some questioning her ability to be a teacher and others throwing hateful *ad hominem* attacks at her. But she stayed the course. Famously, Weil was able to test her "first magnum opus," "Reflections Concerning the Causes of Liberty and Social Oppression," in factories surrounding Paris. Given her early death, it is left to us, her readers in this next century, to essay her second, *The Need for Roots*.

NOTES

1. Aijaz Ahmad, *In Theory: Classes, Nations, Literatures* (New York: Verso, 1992), 1.

2. Joy James, *Resisting State Violence: Radicalism, Gender, and Race in U.S. Culture* (Minneapolis: University of Minnesota Press, 1996), 3.

3. Reed, *Class Notes*, vii.

4. Ibid., viii.

5. Ibid.

6. Ibid., xiii, xiv.

7. Ibid., xiii.

8. Ibid., xiv.

9. Ibid.

10. Ibid., xx.

11. Ibid.

12. Ibid.

13. Ibid.

14. Ibid., xii.
15. Ibid., xxiii.
16. Ibid., xxiv.
17. Bernard Harcourt, *Critique and Praxis* (New York: Columbia University Press, 2020), 4.
18. Ibid., 9.
19. Ibid.
20. Ibid., 10.
21. Ibid., 11.
22. Pétrement, *Simone Weil*, 86
23. Ibid., 96–98.
24. Ibid., 98.
25. Ibid., 103
26. Ibid., 110.
27. Ibid., 111–12.
28. Ibid., 112, 120.

Bibliography

Agamben, Giorgio. "Preface." In Simone Weil, *La personne et le sacré*. Paris: Rivages, 2017.

Ahmad, Aijaz. *In Theory: Classes, Nations, Literatures*. New York: Verso, 1992.

Andic, Martin. "Introduction." In Henry Leroy Finch, *Simone Weil and the Intellect of Grace*. New York: Continuum, 2001.

Andrew, Edward. "Simone Weil on the Injustice of Rights-Based Doctrines." *Review of Politics* 48, no. 1 (1986): 60–91.

Anidjar, Gil. *Blood: A Critique of Christianity*. New York: Columbia University Press, 2014.

Arendt, Hannah. *The Human Condition*. Chicago: University of Chicago Press, 2018.

———. *The Origins of Totalitarianism*. Boston: Mariner, 2001.

Asad, Talal. "What Do Human Rights Do? An Anthropological Enquiry." *Theory & Event* 4, no. 4 (2000).

Berger, John. *Landscapes: John Berger on Art*. New York: Verso, 2016.

———. *Portraits*. New York: Verso, 2017.

Bilgrami, Akeel. *Secularism, Identity, and Enchantment*. Cambridge, MA: Harvard University Press, 2014.

Blanchot, Maurice. *The Infinite Conversation*. Translated by Susan Hanson. Minneapolis: University of Minnesota Press, 1993.

Borgwardt, Elizabeth. *A New Deal for the World: America's Vision for Human Rights*. Cambridge, MA: Harvard University Press, 2007.

Bourgault, Sophie. "Beyond the Saint and the Red Virgin: Simone Weil as Feminist Theorist of Care." *Frontiers* 35, no. 2 (2014): 1–27.

Brown, Wendy. *Regulating Aversion: Tolerance in the Age of Identity and Empire*. Princeton, NJ: Princeton University Press, 2008.

Butler, Judith. *Frames of War: When Is Life Grievable?* New York: Verso, 2009.

Cha, Yoon Sook. *Decreation and the Ethical Bind: Simone Weil and the Claim of the Other*. New York: Fordham University Press, 2017.

Chenavier, Robert. *Simone Weil: Attention to the Real*. Translated by Bernard E. Doering. Notre Dame, IN: University of Notre Dame Press, 2012.

Çubukçu, Ayça. "Thinking Against Humanity." *London Review of International Law* 5, no. 2 (2017): 251–67.

Dargan, Joan. *Simone Weil: Thinking Poetically*. Albany: State University of New York Press, 1999.

Darwish, Mahmoud. *Journal of an Ordinary Grief*. Translated by Ibrahim Muhawi. New York: Archipelago Books, 2010.

Davis, Benjamin P. "The Colonial Frame: Judith Butler and Simone Weil on Force and Grief." In *Simone Weil, Beyond Ideology?* Edited by Sophie Bourgault and Julie Daigle, 125–42. London: Palgrave MacMillan, 2020.

———. "The Politics of Édouard Glissant's Right to Opacity." *CLR James Journal: The Journal of the Caribbean Philosophical Association* 25, nos. 1–2 (2019): 59–70.

———. "The Promises of Standing Rock: Three Approaches to Human Rights." *Humanity: An International Journal of Human Rights, Humanitarianism, and Development* 12, no. 2 (2021): 205–25.

———. "Responsibilities of the Intellectual: Dewey, Dussel, and Democracy." *Inter-American Journal of Philosophy* 11, no. 2 (2020): 35–48.

———. "Simone Weil's Method: Essaying Reality through Inquiry and Action." *Comparative and Continental Philosophy* 13, no. 3 (2021): 235–46.

Davis, Benjamin P., and Eric Aldieri. "Precarity and Resistance: A Critique of Martha Fineman's Vulnerability Theory." *Hypatia* 36, no. 2 (2021): 321–37.

Dean, Jodi. *Comrade: An Essay on Political Belonging*. New York: Verso, 2019.

Derrida, Jacques. *Margins of Philosophy*. Translated by Alan Bass. Chicago: University of Chicago Press, 1982.

Derrida, Jacques, and Anne Dufourmantelle. *Of Hospitality*. Translated by Rachel Bowlby. Stanford: Stanford University Press, 2000.

Dietz, Mary. *Between the Human and the Divine: The Political Thought of Simone Weil*. Totowa, NJ: Rowman & Littlefield, 1988.

Doering, E. Jane. *Simone Weil and the Spectre of Self-Perpetuating Force*. Notre Dame, IN: University of Notre Dame Press, 2010.

Dolezal, Luna, and Danielle Petherbridge. *Body/Self/Other: The Phenomenology of Social Encounters*. Albany: State University of New York Press, 2017.

Dussel, Enrique. *Twenty Theses on Politics*. Translated by George Ciccariello-Maher. Durham, NC: Duke University Press, 2008.

Eiland, Howard, and Michael W. Jennings. *Walter Benjamin: A Critical Life*. Cambridge, MA: Belknap Press of Harvard University Press, 2016.

Eler, Alicia. "Two Young Artists Create a 'Cemetery' in Minneapolis to Honor Victims of Police Killings." *Star Tribune*, June 12, 2020.

Elie, Paul. *The Life You Save May Be Your Own*. New York: Farrar, Straus and Giroux, 2003.

Esposito, Roberto. *The Origin of the Political: Hannah Arendt or Simone Weil?* Translated by Vincenzo Binetti and Gareth Williams. New York: Fordham University Press, 2017.

Fineman, Martha. "Vulnerability and Inevitable Inequality." *Oslo Law Review* 4, no. 3 (2017): 133–49.

Galioto, Katie. "As Chauvin Verdict Looms, Military Presence in Twin Cities Unsettles Some, Reassures Others." *Star Tribune*, April 19, 2021.

Glissant, Édouard. *Poetics of Relation*. Translated by Betsy Wing. Ann Arbor: University of Michigan Press, 1997.

Gordon, Lewis R. *Fear of Black Consciousness*. New York: Farrar, Straus and Giroux, 2022.

Guenther, Lisa. "A Critical Phenomenology of Solidarity and Resistance in 2013 California Prison Hunger Strikes." In *Body/Self/Other: The Phenomenology of Social Encounters*, edited by Luna Dolezal and Danielle Petherbridge, 47–73. Albany: State University of New York Press, 2017.

———. *Solitary Confinement: Social Death and Its Afterlives*. Minneapolis: University of Minnesota Press, 2013.

Gündoğdu, Ayten. *Rightlessness in an Age of Rights: Hannah Arendt and the Contemporary Struggles of Migrants*. New York: Oxford University Press, 2015.

Hadot, Pierre. *Philosophy as a Way of Life: Spiritual Exercises from Socrates to Foucault*. Translated by Michael Chase. Malden, MA: Blackwell, 1995.

Hall, Stuart. *Selected Political Writings*. Edited by Sally Davison et al. Durham, NC: Duke University Press, 2017.

Harcourt, Bernard. *The Counterrevolution: How Our Government Went to War Against Its Own Citizens*. New York: Basic Books, 2018.

———. *Critique and Praxis*. New York: Columbia University Press, 2020.

Hoff, Shannon. "Rights and Worlds: On the Political Significance of Belonging." *Philosophical Forum* 45, no. 4 (2014): 355–73.

Honig, Bonnie. *Public Things: Democracy in Disrepair*. New York: Fordham University Press, 2017.

Hubbard, Kaia. "Outside of Sleeping, Americans Spend Most of Their Time Watching Television." *U.S. News*, July 22, 2021.

James, Joy. *Resisting State Violence: Radicalism, Gender, and Race in U.S. Culture*. Minneapolis: University of Minnesota Press, 1996.

James, Robin. *Resilience & Melancholy: Pop Music, Feminism, Neoliberalism*. Alresford, UK: Zero Books, 2016.

Kinsella, Helen M. "Of Colonialism and Corpses: Simone Weil on Force." In *Women's International Thought: A New History*. Edited by Patricia Owens and Katharina Rietzler. Cambridge: Cambridge University Press, 2021.

Kompridis, Nikolas. *Critique and Disclosure: Critical Theory between Past and Future*. Cambridge, MA: MIT Press, 2006.

Koram, Kojo, and Enrique Prieto-Rios. "Decolonising Epistemologies, Politicising Rights: An Interview with Eduardo Mendieta." *Birkbeck Law Review* 3, no. 1 (2015): 13–31.

Kristeva, Julia. *Strangers to Ourselves*. Translated by Leon S. Roudiez. New York: Columbia University Press, 1991.

Levinas, Emmanuel. *Difficult Freedom: Essays on Judaism*. Translated by Seán Hand. Baltimore: Johns Hopkins University Press, 1990.

Lingis, Alphonso. *Abuses*. Berkeley: University of California Press, 1994.

Lloyd, David, and Paul Thomas. *Culture and the State*. New York: Routledge, 1998.

Lloyd, Vincent. *The Problem with Grace: Reconfiguring Political Theology*. Stanford: Stanford University Press, 2011.

Lugones, María. *Pilgrimages/Peregrinajes: Theorizing Coalition against Multiple Oppressions*. Lanham, MD: Rowman & Littlefield, 2003.

Lyotard, Jean-François. *Why Philosophize?* Translated by Andrew Brown. Cambridge, MA: Polity, 2013.

MacMillen, Sarah. "Faith Beyond Optimism: Simone Weil, Hannah Arendt, and Gillian Rose." *Philosophy and Theology* 23, no. 2 (2011): 257–66.

Mahamud, Faiza. "Among Minnesota's Refugees, Military Presence in Twin Cities Stirs Painful Memories." *Star Tribune*, April 22, 2021.

Maldonado-Torres, Nelson. *Against War: Views from the Underside of Modernity*. Durham, NC: Duke University Press, 2008.

Manke, Shawn. "Minnesota National Guard is Here to Protect People, Their Rights and Their Property." *Star Tribune*, March 7, 2021.

Marx, Karl. *The Economic and Philosophic Manuscripts of 1844*. Translated by Martin Milligan. New York: Prometheus Books, 1988.

McCullough, Lissa. *The Religious Philosophy of Simone Weil: An Introduction*. London: I.B. Tauris, 2014.

———. "Simone Weil's Phenomenology of the Body." *Comparative and Continental Philosophy* 4, no. 2 (2012): 195–218.

McLellan, David. *Utopian Pessimist: The Life and Thought of Simone Weil*. New York: Poseidon, 1990.

Mendieta, Eduardo. *Global Fragments: Globalizations, Latinamericanisms, and Critical Theory*. Albany: State University of New York Press, 2007.

de Menil, Dominique. *The Rothko Chapel: Writings on Art and the Threshold of the Divine*. New Haven, CT: Yale University Press, 2010.

Mignolo, Walter D. *The Darker Side of the Renaissance: Literacy, Territoriality, and Colonization*. Ann Arbor: University of Michigan Press, 1995.

Moyn, Samuel. *Human Rights and the Uses of History*. New York: Verso, 2011.

———. *The Last Utopia: Human Rights in History*. Cambridge, MA: Belknap Press of Harvard University, 2010.

———. "Personalism, Community, and the Origin of Human Rights." In *Human Rights in the Twentieth Century*. Edited by Stefan-Ludwig Hoffman. New York: Cambridge University Press, 2011.

Nagle, Angela. "The Left Case against Open Borders." *American Affairs* 2, no. 4 (2018): 17–30.

Naimou, Angela. *Salvage Work: U.S. and Caribbean Literatures amid the Debris of Legal Personhood*. New York: Fordham University Press, 2015.

Nayar, Jayan. "The Non-Perplexity of Human Rights." *Theory & Event* 22, no. 2 (2019): 267–302.

Nelson, Deborah. *Tough Enough: Arbus, Arendt, Didion, McCarthy, Sontag, Weil*. Chicago: University of Chicago Press, 2017.

Nezhad, Sheila. "Minneapolis Doesn't Need a National Guard Occupation." *Star Tribune*, February 28, 2021.

Nussbaum, Martha. *Political Emotions: Why Love Matters for Justice*. Cambridge, MA: Belknap Press: An Imprint of Harvard University Press, 2013.

Perrin, J. M., and Gustave Thibon. *Simone Weil as We Knew Her.* Translated by Emma Craufurd. New York: Routledge, 1953.

Perugini, Nicola, and Neve Gordon. *The Human Right to Dominate.* New York: Oxford University Press, 2015.

Pétrement, Simone. *Simone Weil: A Life.* Translated by Raymond Rosenthal. New York: Pantheon, 1978.

du Plessix Gray, Francine. *Simone Weil.* New York: Penguin, 2001.

al-Qasim, Samih. "Travel Tickets." In *Victims of a Map: A Bilingual Anthology of Arabic Poetry.* Edited by Abdullah al-Udhari. London: Saqi Books, 1984.

Quijano, Aníbal. "Coloniality of Power, Eurocentrism and Latin America." *Nepantla: Views from the South* 1, no. 3 (2000): 533–58.

Radzins, Inese. "Simone Weil's Social Philosophy: Toward a Post-Colonial Ethic." In *New Topics in Feminist Philosophy of Religion: Contestations and Transcendence Incarnate.* Edited by Pamela Sue Anderson. Dordrecht: Springer, 2010.

Reed Jr., Adolph. *Class Notes: Posing as Politics and Other Thoughts on the American Scene.* New York: New Press, 2001.

Rejack, Brian, and Michael Theune, eds. *Keats's Negative Capability: New Origins and Afterlives.* Liverpool: Liverpool University Press, 2019.

Ricciardi, Alessia. "From Decreation to Bare Life: Weil, Agamben, and the Impolitical." *Diacritics* 39, no. 2 (2009): 75–84, 86–93.

Ritner, Scott B. "Simone Weil's Heterodox Marxism: Revolutionary Pessimism and the Politics of Resistance." In *Simone Weil, Beyond Ideology?* Edited by Sophie Bourgault and Julie Daigle. London: Palgrave Macmillan, 2020.

———. "The Training of the Soul: Simone Weil's Dialectical Disciplinary Paradigm, A Reading alongside Michel Foucault." In *Simone Weil and Continental Philosophy.* Edited by A. Rebecca Rozelle-Stone. London: Rowman & Littlefield International, 2017.

Rose, Jacqueline. "An Endless Seeing." *New York Review of Books,* January 13, 2022.

Rothko, Mark. *Writings on Art.* New Haven, CT: Yale University Press, 2006.

Rozelle-Stone, A. Rebecca. "*Le Déracinement* of Attention: Simone Weil on the Institutionalization of Distractedness." *Philosophy Today* 53, no. 1 (2009): 100–108.

Rozelle-Stone, A. Rebecca, and Lucian Stone. *Simone Weil and Theology.* London: Bloomsbury, 2013.

Said, Edward. *Representations of the Intellectual: The 1993 Reith Lectures.* New York: Vintage, 1994.

Sharpe, Christina. *In the Wake: On Blackness and Being.* Durham, NC: Duke University Press, 2016.

Slaughter, Joseph R. *Human Rights Inc.: The World Novel, Narrative Form, and International Law.* New York: Fordham University Press, 2007.

Smith, Patti. *Devotion.* New Haven, CT: Yale University Press, 2017.

Solnit, Rebecca. *A Field Guide to Getting Lost.* New York: Penguin, 2005.

Sontag, Susan. "Simone Weil." *New York Review of Books,* February 1, 1963.

Spitz, Ellen Handler. *Art and Psyche: A Study in Psychoanalysis and Aesthetics.* New Haven, CT: Yale University Press, 1985.

Spivak, Gayatri Chakravorty. "Can the Subaltern Speak?" In *Colonial Discourse and Post-Colonial Theory*. Edited by Patrick Williams and Laura Chrisman. New York: Columbia University Press, 1994.

Steinbock, Anthony. *Phenomenology and Mysticism: The Verticality of Religious Experience*. Indianapolis: Indiana University Press, 2007.

Stone, Lucian, and Jason Mohaghegh. "Introduction: Outsider Imperatives." In *Manifestos for World Thought*. Edited by Lucian Stone and Jason Bahbak Mohaghegh. Lanham, MD: Rowman & Littlefield International, 2017.

Stonebridge, Lyndsey. *Placeless People: Writing, Rights, and Refugees*. New York: Oxford University Press, 2018.

Terada, Rei. *Feeling in Theory: Emotion after the "Death of the Subject."* Cambridge, MA: Harvard University Press, 2001.

Tully, James. "Political Theory as a Critical Activity." *Political Theory* 30, no. 4 (2002): 533–55.

Vázquez-Arroyo, Antonio Y. *Political Responsibility: Responding to Predicaments of Power*. New York: Columbia University Press, 2016.

Walcott, Rinaldo. *The Long Emancipation: Moving Toward Black Freedom*. Durham, NC: Duke University Press, 2021.

Wampole, Christy. *Rootedness: The Ramifications of a Metaphor*. Chicago: University of Chicago Press, 2016.

Weil, Simone. *On the Abolition of All Political Parties*. Translated by Simon Leys. New York: New York Review of Books, 2013.

———. *La condition ouvrière*. Paris: Éditions Gallimard, 1951.

———. *Écrits historiques et politiques*. Paris: Éditions Gallimard, 1960.

———. *Écrits de Londres et dernières lettres*. Paris: Éditions Gallimard, 1957.

———. *Écrits de Marseille*. Paris: Gallimard, 2008.

———. *Formative Writings: 1929–1941*. Translated by Dorothy Tuck McFarland and Wilhelma Van Ness. Amherst: University of Massachusetts Press, 1987.

———. *Gravity and Grace*. Translated by Emma Crawford and Mario von der Ruhr. New York: Routledge, 2002; *La pesanteur et la grâce*. Paris: Librairie Plon, 1947.

———. *The Need for Roots*. Translated by Arthur Wills. New York: Routledge, 2002; *L'enracinement. Prélude à une déclaration des devoirs envers l'être humain*. Paris: Éditions Gallimard, 1949.

———. *Oppression and Liberty*. Translated by Arthur Wills and John Petrie. New York: Routledge, 1958; *Oppression et Liberté*. Paris: Éditions Gallimard, 1955.

———. *Selected Essays 1934–1943: Historical, Political, and Moral Writings*. Translated by Richard Rees. Eugene, OR: Wipf and Stock, 2015.

———. *Simone Weil on Colonialism*. Translated and edited by J. P. Little. Lanham, MD: Rowman & Littlefield, 2003.

———. *Simone Weil: An Anthology*. New York: Penguin, 2005.

———. *Simone Weil: Late Philosophical Writings*. Translated by Eric O. Springsted and Lawrence E. Schmidt. Notre Dame: University of Notre Dame Press, 2015.

———. *Sur la science*. Paris: Éditions Gallimard, 1966.

———. *Waiting for God*. Translated by Emma Craufurd. New York: Routledge, 2009; *Attente de Dieu*. Paris: Éditions Fayard, 1966.

Whyte, Jessica. "Human Rights and the Collateral Damage of Neoliberalism." *Theory & Event* 20, no. 1 (2017): 137–51.

———. *The Morals of the Market: Human Rights and the Rise of Neoliberalism.* New York: Verso, 2019.

Winch, Peter. *Simone Weil: "The Just Balance."* Cambridge: Cambridge University Press, 1989.

Yountae, An. *The Decolonial Abyss: Mysticism and Cosmopolitics from the Ruins.* New York: Fordham University Press, 2016.

Zaretsky, Robert. "France's Far-Right Claims a Left-Anarchist Martyr as Its Own." *Foreign Policy*, July 30, 2018.

———. "What We Owe to Others: Simone Weil's Radical Reminder." *New York Times*, February 20, 2018.

Index

Abdi, Zaynab, 94
"About the Problems in the French Empire" (Weil), 50n52
abstraction, value of over perception, 13–14
abstract knowledge, concrete action and, 18–19, 31, 131
accident, of factory worker, 34
accomplishments, meanings as, 39
accounting to others, roots as, 101
acting, understanding and, 25–26
action: concrete, 18, 95–96, 132; direct, 130; revolutionary, 132; roots theory contrasted with, 117; U.S. colonial, 46
active consumption, 61, 65–66
activism, 131–32
advertising, 56–57
aesthetics, 18
afflicted people, voices of, 41, 80
affliction *(malheur),* 25, 41
Afghanistan, 102
Ahmad, Aijaz, 129
Allied landing, in north Africa, 96
allies, political contribution of, 121–22
Alsthom Company factory, 20
alternative framing, 39
ambiguity, issues and, 114–15
Amnesty International, 79, 102

Andrew, Edward, 74, 83–84, 88n15
"Antigone" (Weil), 26
Aquinas, Thomas, 108
arbitrary powers, oppression and, 28–29
Arendt, Hannah, 2, 9, 84, 87–88, 116
Aristotle, 108
art, 62–63; politics as, 105, 119–20; of Rothko, 60–61
The Artist's Reality (Rothko), 58–59
Asad, Talal, 86
atopos (out of place), 5–6
attention, concept of Weil, 59, 64
attunement, of Rothko, 59

bad actors, focus on, 78–79
barbarism, forceful and, 43, 43n38
Barber, Anna, 92
Bataille, Georges, 2, 20
beauty, value contrasted with, 57–58
beauty cream example, 57
beings in tension, humans as, 64
belonging, political significance of, 99–100, 118
Benjamin, Walter, 66n5, 107–8
Between the Human and the Divine (Dietz), 3–4, 120
Black people, killed by police, 92
Blanchot, Maurice, 2, 6–7, 65
blood, emphasis on by Weil, 40, 49n31

141

About the Author

Benjamin P. Davis is a postdoctoral fellow in the Department of African American Studies at Saint Louis University. He holds a PhD in Philosophy from Emory University. He is the author of *Choose Your Bearing: Édouard Glissant, Human Rights, and Decolonial Ethics* (Edinburgh UP, 2023) and the coeditor of the forthcoming volume *Creolizing Critical Theory: New Voices in Caribbean Philosophy*, also from Rowman & Littlefield. Davis's research that brings together questions of human rights and decolonial thinking includes the articles "What Could Human Rights Do? A Decolonial Inquiry" (*Transmodernity*, 2020); "The Promises of Standing Rock" (*Humanity*, 2021); and "Human Rights and Caribbean Philosophy: Implications for Teaching" (*Journal of Human Rights Practice*, 2021). Their additional writings on Weil include the article "A/theologies of the Impossible: Antigone, Weil, Badiou, and the Strange" (*Journal for Cultural and Religious Theory*, 2017). Davis is a member of the Caribbean Philosophical Association and the Vice President of the American Weil Society. He has also written several public-facing essays on politics for *Public Seminar*. His writing can be found on his website: https://benjaminpdavis.com/.